Glasgow's Central Station was almost deserted. The kiosks and newsstands, denuded of their wares, reminded Bruce, appropriately enough, of the graveyard in Aribaig. Thinking of home brought a tightening to his throat, but he forced it back.

Even such longing for his home was as nothing to the sadness he felt now for what he had just forfeited. Lifting his head up, he felt himself droop with tiredness and dejection. Never again to hear Jean speak his name in that special way she had tonight for the first time. Shy and sweet yet sure. Instead, the echo of her scream resounded through his head, filling him with renewed horror: "You've killed my father!"

Call of the Isles is the compelling story of Bruce MacAlister, a crofter's son who is called to the ministry. Offering romance, adventure, and intrigue, this novel shows in an engaging manner what it means to trust God wholeheartedly.

Call of the Isles

MOLLY GLASS

Power Books

Fleming H. Revell
Old Tappan, New Jersey

Scripture quotations in this volume are based on the King James Version of the Bible.

Library of Congress Cataloging-in-Publication Data

Glass, Molly.
  Call of the Isles / Molly Glass.
    p. cm.
  ISBN 0-8007-5290-2
  I. Title.
  PS3557.L345C3 1989
  813'.54—dc19

88-30189
CIP

Copyright © 1989 by Molly Glass
Published by the Fleming H. Revell Company
Old Tappan, New Jersey 07675
Printed in the United States of America

Call of the Isles

1

Squeezing his eyes tight shut to keep the tears in and the dark out, four-year-old Bruce MacAlister turned his face to the wall. The darkness was so thick and black, and oh, how he wished his gran'pa would hurry up and come to bed, because he had so much to ask him. First he wanted to know what Faither would be doing in heaven, and if heaven was really down there in that big hole in the ground, and. . . . Shuddering, Bruce clutched his shawl. Earlier his mam had tucked it round him as usual, but tonight she had not stayed to tell him a story. Pressing the familiar shawl into his mouth and biting down hard on it helped, and soon the shivering stopped. The attic steps squeaked, and Bruce sat up quickly, wide awake again, eyes turned expectantly toward the door. Now he would find out, because Gran'pa knew everything!

Carefully balancing the oil lamp to light the narrow steps, the old man made his way slowly, knowing the laddie would be waiting with the questions. He had been delaying this moment, because they would be questions he, too, would like to have answered. However he had just finished trying to console Elspeth, and now he must do his best to help young Bruce understand what he himself failed to. If life was to go on, as it must, even if they could not understand it, they could at least be reconciled to it. Sighing, he opened the door.

". . . And so ye see, the Lord disna dae things like that. Your faither will be someplace where it is light, in fact brighter than we know. As for breathin', I'm sure he'll have nae need to be worrit' aboot that either. Never forget, Brucie, nae matter what anybody tells ye, your faither was a guid man! The Maker will understan', I'm quite sure. You and me and, aye, yer mother as well, might have thought your faither did some strange things, but we must ken he had his reasons. A' the same, the best way is tae trust the Lord. We have tae carry on and make the best o' it. Get tae sleep now, laddie; the mornin'll be here soon enough, and we'll still have the milkin' tae do. The kye'll no' wait till we've slept in."

Elspeth MacAlister had learned in a hard school that crying over spilt milk did no good, so she was all the more surprised when the unbidden tears sprang to her eyes now as she found herself making four places at the breakfast table. Quickly snatching up the extra piggin of porridge, before her keen-eyed son made mention of it, she spoke sharply to hide her confusion: "Hurry up and eat your porridge so that we can get to the milking. That Star has been bawling away for the last ten minutes, and who can blame the beast?"

As the three made their way to the milking shed the habits of years came foremost. Bruce, small as he was, had his jobs to do, and he worked willingly enough. His mother, sitting milking Star with no need to concentrate on her actions, allowed her thoughts to return to yesterday's graveside service. Watching the six men lower their burden into the waiting earth, that burden so recently a living man, her man, John, she had stood firm and tearless.

The awareness that a woman at a graveside, it not being the custom, would therefore be frowned upon by most of her neighbors had not deterred her from her place there. What did it matter now what they thought? What did anything matter now? Her answer to that came as her son slipped his small hand into hers. It mattered for Bruce. She would face anything for her son. Poor John was gone from them; Bruce would one day show them all that his father's life had not been for nothing.

If only John hadn't been such a one for taking everything to heart, as if he alone were at fault for the ills of the world. What was that phrase in Latin he always murmured when something upset him? Mea culpa, *yes, that was it. If he had not been so grim about life, he would still be here today, sitting milking Star while I did my own jobs in the house.* The warm, white liquid frothed and splashed into her pail as she worked. It was brim full now, and the cow turned its head to throw her a look of mild protest.

Elspeth found herself whispering to the indignant animal: "Oh, I know I haven't John's touch, Star, and I'm sorry, but you'll just have to make the best of it, like all the rest of us!" Taking the pail to the cooler for emptying, her eyes filled again. *I really must get hold of myself. This is a poor example for Bruce and distresses the old man.* Leaving them to finish up, she returned to the house. Soon they would come in, famished and ready for the ham and eggs and griddle scones she would have hot for them. Gran'pa Bruce, as she affectionately called her father-in-law, liked a cup of strong, scalding tea to wash it all down. After that the minister was coming back to continue the discussion about the future of the MacAlister family, where they had left off last night. Today it must be settled.

The Reverend Fraser Clegg practiced what he preached. As a result he was not always understood or, if understood, not always appreciated either by his colleagues in the "kirk" or his parishioners in the small Scottish township of Aribaig. His wife, Janet, also seldom understood him, but she loved him and at day's end would be his listening post.

"John was a good man, Janet!" Having heard this, or its equivalent, many times in the last few days, the wise Janet said nothing but continued to unlace his boots.

"Yes, what I still cannot fathom is the way he would talk to me at great length about the subjects that bothered him, but the minute I mentioned anything he thought might be leading to religion, he would get up and walk away!" Knowing how these thoughts grieved her man, Janet sighed as she finished removing his boots, praying all the while he would just let go. Oblivious to her ministrations, even when she loosened his collar and began kneading the back of his neck where it was as tight as a drum, he still seemed unheeding. It was not that Janet didn't sympathize with the MacAlisters, indeed she did, but she had heard much of this before. She knew better than to interrupt him, however, so she kept on rubbing gently.

"Many's the grand talk we did have of an evening, John and me, before the drink got the better of him. Although a lot of his words were not the kind I could ever repeat in the pulpit, I still enjoyed listening to him."

"Do you think them to be true then?" Janet ventured. "The stories he told, I mean. After all, I couldn't help overhearing some of them, when you brought him home to the manse."

"Oh, maybe not every word. John had a way with words, as you know, but I ken the basis of what he said would be true enough. How he would go on when he got worked up about his ancestry, for instance." Fraser's brogue thickened when he became excited.

"I remember! Why, the very last time he was here, we got the whole story of that as if he was proud of it!"

"He certainly showed no shame whatever, but after all, it could hardly be called his fault . . . ," Fraser's eyes began to take on the glassy, faraway look his wife knew only too well, so with barely a sigh, she subsided at his feet, hoping this story held something she might not have heard before. Whatever it would be, she sensed his need to speak.

"As I recall, it was a very cold night, and you were ben making us a hot drink. As usual my honest friend grumbled away about the drinks having no whiskey, but I, priding myself on being just as honest, reminded him that he still came to visit us, knowing the drinks would be dry. Here is what he said: 'Och, yes, Fraser, my fine, upstandin', ecclesiastical friend, there are more things in life than the drink, even for me. I come for the good talk and of course the good listener, yourself! As I've told you before, it was few friends I had at the academy, I cared to consort with. Being the bastard son of a crofter's daughter, even if the father was a ClanRanald, did not put me in the top of the social set exactly!' and that was him started. He went on to tell me how his mother was given in marriage to Bruce MacAlister, a grand fellow who was tackmaster to the 'Ranald. They were set up on the farm here in Aribaig as a reward to MacAlister for marrying Morag Campbell and taking on her unborn. John always laughed at that, because apparently his step-father needed no such encouragement, as he cared much for Morag. Being the good, thrifty Scot he was, he could not refuse such bounty. Bounty indeed! The 'Ranald's pride in his manly ability to further the species allowed him to acknowl-edge his many offspring by ensuring they were well provided for."

"He must have been very rich, the ClanRanald!" Janet had returned to her love task of massaging the back of her husband's neck. Since he was beginning to wind down now, she knew that soon he would notice her. He did!

"You are quite right, my love; we'll just leave it with the Lord. I may not understand, but then I wonder if I need to." The wise young wife, herself wondering what she had been quite right about, said no more, and soon they forgot about the MacAlisters for a time.

Next morning, however, as he stood looking down at the fatherless boy Fraser Clegg was sharply reminded again of his friend John. The boy was his father's "double" as they would say in the village. In certain lights and conditions Fraser saw the softer look of the mother, Elspeth, but today the fine brows and square forehead, creased with many questions, imaged John's. Realizing they were all waiting for him, Fraser came back to the situation at hand.

". . . So you see, Mrs. MacAlister, John told me to give you this if ever anything should happen to him!" The piece of yellow parchment the reverend now held out meant little to

Elspeth, even after it was spread out on the cleared kitchen table. The curlicues and curves of the fading black marks on the ancient scrip were just that to her, black marks! Elspeth MacAlister's extraordinary reading ability, nurtured by her father since her fourth birthday, deserted her now as the ornate copperplate writing began to blur before her eyes and her emotions once more played her traitor.

"Will you read it to us, minister, please? I'd be much obliged!"

"I'll do better than that, Mrs. MacAlister, and be glad to. I'll tell you what it appears to mean." Fraser's voice, intoning the official words on the insurance policy, droned on and on as he read every word down to the smallest print.

"Could I be understanding you right then? Do I get six hundred pounds?"

"That would appear to be what it says, and as far as I can ascertain, it is perfectly in order, yes!" Fraser was now speaking in what his wife called his "pulpit" voice, something carefully nourished at Glasgow University; but he took great pains to disguise this whenever he remembered. Summing up for the two intent adults, the junior member of the group having fallen asleep long ago, Fraser continued: "The document states quite clearly that the widow of John Keir MacAlister would receive six hundred pounds sterling on the occasion of his demise, providing his death was from natural causes." He glanced over to the older MacAlister as he said that, but Bruce, Senior, only gazed down at the boy on his lap. "All you need do is take or send this paper to the Edinburgh address on the heading, and my advice is that you go in person. In fact don't let it out of your sight until you have the money in your hand. Don't sign any papers, either, before they give you the money." Following this statement, silence reigned in the warm kitchen, except for the familiar sound of the grandfather clock as it ticked importantly in the corner. A bit of coal gave a small explosion in the shining fireplace. Each person there had become busy with thoughts too deep for utterance here and now.

At last Elspeth spoke, addressing her father-in-law. "Gran'pa Bruce, it would not be wrong then for us to save the bit of money for the boy. With him going to be a minister himself someday, God willing!"

"No my dear, it would not be wrong. It would be very right!" A fleeting smile of complete accord passed between the two who had loved John MacAlister but who both had to stand helplessly by while he destroyed himself. "The de'il meant it for evil, but God will use it for good!"

"Amen!"

"Amen!" Fraser's hearty response woke the boy, and as he sat up, rubbing his eyes, he heard his mother say, "Would you please say a word o' prayer, minister?"

"I will indeed! Dear God, those of us gathered here in this place today, all so fond of our dear departed brother, ask you to blot from our memory any unworthy thoughts we might be harboring. Help those of us who are older to cherish and protect this young life so that no shadow of his father's life or untimely death will ever cloud his being. Bless this home we pray now and all who reside and enter here. In the name of our Lord and Savior Jesus Christ. Amen."

{ 2 }

Speeding toward the city of her birth, Elspeth MacAlister found she had no tears left to waste on Edinburgh.
Opposite her, crunched up tightly in the corner seat of the
railway carriage, Bruce watched her intently. Pleased at how
calm she felt and stiffening her resolve to have done with
regrets, Elspeth smiled brightly on her son. They would turn
this experience into an adventure.

"Is that not a fine view we're getting, son?" Bruce at once sat
up obediently and shifted his gaze to the scenery rushing past
the windows. He watched quietly for a while, and she smiled
again, this time at the creases furrowing his brow. Soon he
would have a question.

"Where are the isles, Mam? I don't see any isles!"

"What kind of daft question is that, Bruce? Gran'pa explained
to you how we would first go on a stagecoach to Fort William,
and then the train would take us across Scotland, to Edinburgh.
Why he even drew you a wee map the same as the one in the
minister's book." She pulled the crumpled map out of her son's
pocket as she spoke, smoothing it before them.

"Oh, yes, I know, Mam, but I thought there would be isles in
the sea, the same as at home!" His eyes sought the lines in the
map as he tried to understand.

"Son, I don't know what you mean! When we get to
Edinburgh, we'll be close to the sea. Not as close as we are at

home in Aribaig, I'll grant, but there is water called the Firth of Forth that goes right through like. Here, I'll show you." She was guiding his finger over the roughly drawn map. "Look, this is where we started, and this is where we went on the stagecoach. Then, when we got to Fort William, we changed to the train, and here we are, still on the train. All day we've not had a glimpse of the sea, but I promise you tomorrow we'll go to a place where you'll get a sight and a smell of it again."

For a wee boy not yet five years old the geography lesson must seem hard, so Elspeth waited for more questions.

"Oh, yes, I see now, Mam! The isles are just bits of Scotland broken off, like an oatcake, and when the water seeps in like this," pointing to the Firth, "it's still a'thegither!" Elspeth laughed aloud.

"Your father would be proud of you, Brucie, and he could not have said it better. What will we do now? We still have a while before we get to Waverley Station."

"Could I have an oatcake, Mam? I'm blessed if I'm not hungry!" Laughing again at this euphemism, which sounded exactly like Gran'pa Bruce, Elspeth reached for the picnic basket on the overhead rack. His mother's laugh reassured Bruce that everything was all right again. As he bit into the oatcake, generously spread with thick farm butter and a chunk of cheese, the train plunged into a tunnel.

Elspeth's softly whispered words were drowned out by the shrieking whistle, "The king is dead! Long live the king!"

Still smiling, she began to point out renowned landmarks as they appeared, and by the time the train slowed down to enter the unfinished yet already teaming station at Edinburgh's heart, the atmosphere sparkled with their shared excitement.

The patter of rain on the tiled roof woke them the next morning. Vaguely comforting to Elspeth, the unfamiliar sound, along with the clip-clop of horses' hooves clattering on the cobbled street outside, caused Bruce to jump out of bed and run across the room to investigate. Stretching as high as he could, he could still see nothing but clouds through the tiny window. Grasping the windowsill with two small hands, he lifted himself barely to its level.

"Oh, look, Mam! Is that the castle? It looks more like Paddy the Packman's bald head, covered with his tam-o'-shanter." True to her resolve to leave futile regrets behind, Elspeth smiled at the childish joke. Turning from tidying the bed, she peered out through the streaming windowpane.

"I believe you're right, Brucie. It does remind you of Paddy, but come on, we're wasting time. We've got a lot of things to do and see today, even if it *is* raining!" Before Bruce could ask what things, there was a knock on the door. Elspeth opened it to find a serving maid balancing a tray, heavy with a giant teapot and a plate full of oatcakes. The butter melting and oozing onto the dish, from the steaming hot bannocks, might have been from her own churning. Quickly Elspeth brushed away the nostalgia that threatened to overcome her, and greatly daring, she handed the girl a silver threepence from her precious hoard. Wide eyed and wondering, Bruce watched as the maid slipped the coin into the pocket of her petticoat, having first tested it with her teeth.

The MacAlisters collapsed in a heap on the bed, after that, subsiding into the room's one and only chair. At last Elspeth drew in a deep breath as she said, "We'll be good now and start behaving as if we were seasoned travelers. When our business is all attended to, we will go and have a fine dinner at a restaurant and then . . . oh, why do we not just wait and see?"

The deep longing within to go and visit her mother and her old home was so vivid that Elspeth almost cried it aloud. Even just thinking about it caused her heart to start thumping at such a rate she became fearful. Bruce, hopping from one foot to the other, was impatient to begin.

"Hurry up, Mam, it's stopped rainin', and the sun's comin' out now, and I see it winkin' and blinkin' on that big rock yonder, chasin' the clouds. Can we go now, Mam? Please, can we?"

*   *   *

"Mr. Webb will see you now, Mrs. MacAlister." The speaker, a clerk with the Amicable Insurance Company, and the fourth one to have spoken to them during the past hour, motioned Elspeth toward the door leading to the inner sanctum: the office of the great man himself. Mr. Webb, no less than the senior underwriter for the company, would now consider her claim. Leaving Bruce in the care of clerk number four, Elspeth entered into the "presence." A distinct feeling that she should bow to the austere personage facing her across the enormous desk came over her. Fascinated, she watched the man make a bridge of his fingertips, his elbows resting on the blotting pad.

"Have a chair, Mrs. MacAlister." Sweeping his hand in an arc as though bestowing a great favor upon her, he indicated the papers on his desk. "Everything seems to be in order here, except for one detail." Elspeth expelled a long-held breath and waited. "We will require a doctor's certificate, in addition to the one you have here, stating specifically that your husband's death was normal." The man's words, spoken so casually, tore through her. How could the untimely demise of a man of thirty-six be considered normal? Not trusting herself to speak, she waited for Mr. Webb to continue. "It would be indeed unfortunate if an accident or misdemeanor caused the death of John Keir MacAlister!"

"Just what do you mean, sir?" An unusual sharpness entered Elspeth's voice as the whole sorry matter washed over her emotions again. The morning's resolutions to keep cheerful no matter what fled swiftly. Why, not so much as a fortnight ago, her man John had been alive, and the existence of this office, the clerks outside the door, and even the great Mr. Webb himself, with his hints and insinuations, mattered nothing to the MacAlister family.

"Well, mistress, in the case of accidental death or death by misdemeanor, we would only be liable to pay ten percent of the benefit, which in this case would be sixty pounds!" Seething inside but outwardly calm as she remembered Fraser's warnings, Elspeth reached over to pick up the paper before answering.

"Thank you very much, Mr. Webb. I'll let you know." Outside the room she rushed blindly to where a completely gullible Bruce stood, mouth agape, having listened avidly for the past half hour to such good stories that he could hardly wait to tell his mother about them. She didn't stop to hear anything or even thank the young man who had provided the entertainment. Reaching the street, she slowed down only slightly.

One sentence of Bruce's blethers came through her tumbled thoughts of whether to try for the needed certificate and risk opening up some kind of Pandora's box or whether to settle the matter with sixty pounds and be done with it.

"The picture on the wall did so talk, Mam, it did so! I saw the eyes move, and the man, his name is Jimmy, says I'm a braw lad and would someday be famous mysel' and would cross the ocean and do great exploits, and—"

Elspeth exploded: "Great exploits. Great exploits, indeed! I'm surprised at them putting ideas like that into your head."

Sensing quickly that the mood of the morning had somehow gone, Bruce stopped his chattering and waited. They seated themselves in the tearoom as planned. As the food was placed before them Elspeth spoke into the silence: "I'm sorry, son, we are still going to have this bit of a holiday, and we'll enjoy it the best way we can. As your father himself would say, 'It's a' the same now!' We will stay in Edinburgh for a day or two more, and I'll show you the town as I remember it myself. Come on now, eat up your dinner, and after that we'll make up our minds what to do next. What would you like? There's the zoo, or. . . ."

Even as she said it, Elspeth MacAlister knew that the plan, simmering in her heart since the minute Fraser mentioned Edinburgh, had evolved to the place where she would put it into practice. She would take Bruce to see her mother. The problem concerning the insurance money could wait. Maybe even her father . . . but no, that would be too much to hope for. Hugh Edward Munro, barrister and solicitor, her father and a man of strict routine, was always in his office at this hour of the day, so they would go to her old home and take a chance. The trams still ran to Morningside; she had noticed one earlier as they made their way to the insurance office. Could that only have been an hour ago?

Walking through the wrought-iron gateway and up the familiar path to the house, Elspeth almost changed her mind. Heart in mouth, she hesitated: *What if?* Lifting her chin, she steadied herself. Having come this far, she would finish it out. Bruce had hardly spoken since she announced her decision; he had reverted to the uneasy watching she had noticed in the train. During the shaky, clanking journey on the horse tram, she herself had chattered all the way, only stopping now as they approached the formidable-looking door. The shiny brass knocker, shaped like a clenched fist, still dominated the heavy oak panels facing them. Resolutely Elspeth grasped it and let it fall. The noise echoed and re-echoed through the silence like a thunderclap. Maybe they were out! Maybe they wouldn't answer. Suddenly the door opened a crack, and a pair of inquiring eyes appeared in the space. Then it was flung violently back, and Elspeth found herself enveloped in a massive embrace.

"Miss Elspeth, it's yersel', and this is never your laddie? But aye, it is him! I can see the look o'—" But before the speaker could delve further into Bruce's ancestry, another voice reached the small group, which still stood on the doorstep.

"Who is it, Aggie?" As Elspeth and her mother faced each other, five years vanished. At first glance, nothing seemed changed at all, but quickly the deep pain of her mother's inner suffering welled up between the two. Swaying slightly at the sight of her daughter and the child, Margaret Munro quickly grasped the banister behind her, struggling for a second to collect her thoughts. Here indeed stood her well-beloved only child, the same child her husband had banished and who could never be mentioned in his presence. Swearing an oath on the big family Bible, from which he had just torn out the page containing Elspeth's name, Hugh Munro had declared that never would the person, up to then known as Elspeth Falkirk Munro, darken his door again. Until this moment she never had. As the four people stood looking at one another, two inside the lintel and two out, the little human tableau became a scene out of time itself, one of those moments remembered forever by the players.

Aggie broke the spell: "We mauna staun here on the doorstep, Mrs. Munro, ma'am. The neighbors are gawkin' as it is!" With a candor of an old family retainer, she continued, "Should we no' go inside, and I'll mask some tea?" Shocked into a decision, Margaret Munro inclined her head.

"Come in!" As the door closed behind them she thought, *What can he do to me?* and then immediately, *Whatever he does, it will be worth it!*

$\cdot\cdot\circ\cdot\{\,3\,\}\cdot\circ\cdot$

The "tea" that Aggie spread before them turned out to be one of her famous feasts. Fresh scones and tiny, feathery pancakes swathed in butter and homemade strawberry jam, followed by slices of rich, fruity cherry cake and shortbread fingers, were all as good as only Aggie could bake. Elspeth's throat tightened in a desperate effort not to cry again, this time for joy. Bruce had no such inhibitions, and the delights of the fine feed helped him overcome his first feelings of shyness. Having answered the usual questions about name and age, through a mouth stuffed with food, Bruce was glad his mother seemed not to be noticing. She was too busy talking to the old lady dressed in black to see and scold him for his bad manners. The old lady, his grandmother of course, was making the most of her time. Under no illusion that it could ever be repeated, she thanked a kind and wise providence for allowing her this oasis in the desert of her life. Barring a miracle, she knew the outcome of today's visit. The fleeting hope that the child might possibly be an instrument of reconciliation quickly evaporated as she gazed her fill at him. What a fine boy, with his Celtic looks. She detected a little bit of Elspeth but mostly the MacAlister.

Margaret loved Bruce so much already that the pain became almost too hard to bear. The stamp of the father stood out plain for all to see. Even if that made no difference to her, Hugh would catch it at once. Nevertheless she decided to take this gift

21

of a few hours of joy and cherish every minute as though it were the last, knowing it very well could be.

For all that, Margaret still found it difficult to express her feelings, but Elspeth, knowing her mother well, watched as she paused behind Bruce and placed a soft white hand on his head, absentmindedly pushing back the lock of shiny hair that always fell straight down in front of his eyes.

Thinking this was just like being in church, Bruce sat very still, unaware of the drama but knowing instinctively not to draw away. Instead he said, "Mr. Clegg kens that, too, he's the minister in Aribaig!" His remark caused a mild burst of laughter from both women, and as Aggie reentered the room, supposedly to clear the tea but really to feast her eyes on the visitors, she must be told the joke, and the last of the awkwardness vanished. Encouraged, Bruce started to tell his delighted audience the story of Jimmy Carmichael, the would-be ventriloquist, although he didn't know that word, and Aggie, giving up all pretense of work, perched on the edge of the sofa to listen. Her hearty laugh rang out, joined by the more refined tones of her mistress and Elspeth, both laughing through their pain.

Into this setting, at precisely his usual hour of five o'clock, freed from his day's toil in the courts, marched the omnipotent head of the household, Hugh Munro himself.

Hanging up his cape on the fine oaken rack, which he never failed to admire anew every time he used it, Hugh's concentration wavered only slightly as he caught sight of the strange coat on one of the ornate pegs. Strange, yet somehow familiar, and he did not need the confirmation of the smaller jacket or the bonnet of MacAlister tartan beside it to tell him who was visiting.

"No!" The word exploded at the same time as the realization that even this conceded an acknowledgment not to be tolerated. The child of his body and the only fruit of his wife's womb had died for him on the day she told him of John MacAlister. In utterly defying all he, Hugh Munro, considered holy, that day she died to him. Not even a short time of mourning would he allow himself or the two women left in his household. After a few feeble attempts to mention the forbidden name, they had at last come to accept that he meant what he said. For him, no such person existed! During the course of his business encounters, colleagues and employees had, through some extremely embarrassing and uncomfortable moments, realized that Munro was childless in his own heart. One jovial and kindly old judge, who knew Elspeth and whom she addressed as uncle, persisted in asking him questions for a while. He, too, gave up one day after receiving a blank stare as if he had not spoken. Not to be outdone, Judge Nicol had his own way of dealing with such things and only a few days ago in the judges' retiring room had announced in a loud voice: "Was that not a sad case, John MacAlister of Aribaig to be dead so suddenly, and him only thirty-six? Do you recall him when he was here, reading for the law?" The person Judge Nicol accosted with the question had no idea that the old man meant the information for the ears of Counselor Munro, but Munro knew.

His hardness was untouched then, and today, as he entered his study, his place of retreat from a sorry world, it was still intact. His actions were no different from any other night; he would read the paper as he warmed himself at the fire. He removed his boots and put on his slippers before ringing the bell for Aggie.

The occupants of the kitchen, cozy and enclosed in a cocoon of time and space, knew at once the dream was ended. No one else rang a bell quite like that.

Shocked into quick action, Aggie, thinking of the empty grate, wailed, "Oh, my lands, the Maister, and I forgot the time, nae fire in his study!" She rushed out the door as she spoke. Mother and daughter gazed long at each other. Both knew well enough what that bell signified. To Margaret it said, "What is different about tonight, except that Aggie is becoming slothful? Maybe we should pension her off." To Elspeth it confirmed her nonbeing in her father's eyes. To the young boy, who knew nothing of all this drama, it was a summons not to be ignored. Deciding to go after this newfound friend, who had been giving him such tender attention all afternoon, he ran out of the kitchen in time to see Aggie's skirt disappearing into a room further down the hall. He quickly followed.

". . . And so, Aggie, we'll overlook it this time, but maybe it is a good notion to keep at the back of your mind. We are all getting on in years, and it is no big shame to be absent-minded. . . ." His voice faltered only slightly as he caught the movement of the child entering his sanctum. The lapse was fleeting, and quickly gathering his resolve again, he continued to discourse to Aggie about her soon retirement. She, blinded with the tears streaming down her face, was having great difficulty in lighting the fire. In his plan to disregard the boy, Hugh Munro reckoned without Bruce. Taught his manners by Elspeth and taught to be friendly by his Gran'pa MacAlister, Bruce now walked toward this newcomer, one small hand extended.

"How do you do, sir, my name is Bruce MacAlister. I'll be five on my next birthday and . . . ," hesitating at the lack of response, the childish voice faltered. A piece of kindling burst with a crackle and a hiss; the wall clock chimed the quarter hour. No other sound could be heard while they waited. This boy, who looked so like the roué Hugh Munro hated with a dreadful, consuming passion, was still a part of Elspeth, too. Munro's traitor mind, hard and always the lawyer's as it undoubtedly was, still refused to blank out the thought that the boy before him was also a part of himself.

"You'll do that then, Aggie. You'll write to your brother in Arbroath, I mean?" Aggie gasped. Not stopping to gather the tools, she rushed from the study as she realized what the man planned to do. *The "maister" went too far this time!*

"No, Mr. Munro, sir, I'll no' write him, I'll go the now, this very day. Indeed that I will!" Bruce could not understand. Response to his offer of a handshake was usually a broad smile with a hand, often rough and calloused, enfolding his small one. The puzzled look crossed his face, leaving furrows from the hairline to the nose. This characteristic of the grandfather in front of him was lost on the man now turning and tending the fire for himself. The moment of weakness vanished forever.

Bruce backed up to the door. His mother, shaking and trembling, having heard a garbled version from Aggie, gathered him up, and not stopping to put on the coats hastily snatched from the oak stand, Elspeth plunged through the front door and bolted blindly down the path. For the second time that day, she became heedless of where her headlong dash would take them. Instinct drew her toward a brightly lit window that seemed to beckon away at the end of the street. That the beam came from the "den of iniquity" long ago forbidden and banned by her father crossed her mind, but she laughed wildly. Elspeth Munro was long past caring. What he thought would never again be a concern of hers or of her son. Safely inside the Crossroads Inn, the friendly warmth rose up to meet her, causing her to stumble forward, almost fainting. She was caught up by the startled landlord. Quickly he called for his wife, and soon, feeling completely restored, Elspeth sat up and looked about her, thankful to be engulfed by the pulsations of human kindness. In a minute she would ask the landlord to send a lad for a cabby. Then she, Elspeth MacAlister, would take herself and her child far away from this place, never to return.

Sunday afternoons in the farmhouse had fallen into a certain routine, and today was no exception. Bruce would read aloud to the family, gathered round the fireplace. On this particular Sunday he was reading from the book *Curiosities of London Life*, and it seemed to be enthralling all but one of his audience.

"It says here: '. . . The deep gorge of a railway cutting, which has ploughed through the center of the market gardens, burrowing beneath carriage roads, flattening a thousand houses out of its path, pursues a circuitous course to the city!' Does that seem fair to you, Gran'pa? All those folks being left with no houses!"

"No, not a bit fair, laddie, but then the highland clearances werena' fair either. Ye'll find there's not much fair in this world between the haves and the have-nots. The word they use is *progress*, and we're no' against that, but the truth is siller talks, and the gentry listen. Some of them have money invested in the Great Western Railways, and that is what they measure by." Elspeth listened absently to her son and his grandfather, but her attention centered more on the other occupants of the front room.

Only work absolutely necessary could be done on Sunday. Andrew, her husband of nearly eight years now, was very strict about that. Andrew Cormack, a man new to the village, had asked Elspeth to marry him less than a year after the "visit" to Edinburgh. It would ever be called the "visit," because Elspeth solemnly vowed that she would never again return to the city where she had suffered so much pain and embarrassment. She had hardly hesitated before giving Andrew her answer, concluding it would be a most sensible solution. So they had married quietly in the manse vestry, and Andrew, along with his son, Hamish, had become part of the household.

After fleeing her father's house that terrible day, Elspeth and Bruce had stayed in the warm shelter of the inn until the arrival of a cabbie. Before it came, they had been joined by a breathless but determined Aggie, and they had traveled together to the city. Aggie had remained with them until morning, when they had again shared a cabbie to Waverley Station. Then Aggie had left for Arbroath, while a still-bewildered Bruce and his mother had taken the first train to Fort William. A tearful Aggie had obtained Elspeth's promise that she would write, and although the maid's literary ability was limited, she in turn had promised to keep in touch with her old mistress, thereby passing on any news from each to the other.

As for the Amicable Insurance Company, Elspeth had written to them and in due course received their reply. A year had passed before the conclusion of the matter. Mr. Webb and his associates concluded that John Keir MacAlister had met his death by misadventure. With the letter came their regrets that, in the circumstances, they could only settle for 10 percent of the death benefit. By then Elspeth had said yes to Andrew.

When the money had arrived, Andrew had insisted the Bank of Scotland be informed that this sixty pounds was put by in trust for young Bruce. There it would earn interest and be even more useful to him when the time came for university. When Andrew had done this, it had brought further proof to Elspeth that she and her husband shared the same hopes for the boy, Bruce. He would be a minister!

During the troubles in northeastern Scotland over sheep land, about the time of the "visit," Andrew's own croft had fallen under a tyrant squire whose demands had forced the Cormacks to leave. So when they arrived in Aribaig, following Elspeth's return, Andrew had applied to his cousin Bruce MacAlister for work and not long after had proposed to Elspeth.

Hamish, seventeen years old at the time, had not been as pleased with the arrangement as Andrew, but his father had not consulted him, so it happened.

No words of romance had passed between the couple, and on the surface it appeared to be a strictly business arrangement. The two had soon developed a respect for one another, and as the years passed, a deeper regard surfaced on occasion. As they completely agreed with Gran'pa Bruce on Bruce's future, that had left Hamish, if not exactly out of the picture, at best only on the edge.

The household then was a quiet, peaceful one for the most part. If times came when a lack of intellectual stimulation and excitement dulled Elspeth's days, she never remarked or complained. They had enough food, warm shelter, and a few sovereigns in the kist. Reflecting on it all, this rainy Sunday afternoon, Elspeth's sigh registered a goodly measure of contentment. There was something satisfying in having predictable Sundays, or any days for that matter.

Bruce's reading had ended, and Elspeth glanced up from her knitting. Three of the four men were expectantly waiting for her to respond to something she had missed. Staring blankly, she said, "What did you say, son? I missed that." A gust of laughter greeted this remark, and soon all three were laughing as a still-puzzled Elspeth looked on in confusion. The joke was on her, apparently, but no explanation was forthcoming.

Hamish did not join in the merriment. At twenty-five years old, although he always appeared content enough, he really felt the opposite. Not in the least interested in the reading and unable to read for himself, he usually just waited, but today discontent welled up inside him. His thoughts centered upon the contents of the kist, at this moment underneath him. His stepmother, although he could never think of her as anything but Mrs. MacAlister, had very ingeniously turned the big wooden chest into a couch by sewing a quilted cover and fitting it round the thing. Hamish had his mind on the bag of sovereigns he had watched his father place in it after the market last week, when they had sold a heifer. No one had said so, but Hamish guessed the money would be for Bruce. Everything went into the kist and then into the bank for Bruce! Why should he, Hamish, not have some of the extra money for a change? All that talk from the old man about the haves and the have-nots! What did they think he was? Squirming, because sitting still for so long was anathema to him at any time, he came to a decision. Leaping to his feet, without a word he lifted the latch from the door and plunged out into the night, not bothering to close the door behind him. A flurry of cold rain and wind swept through the outer room, and the peat fire belched a great cloud of smoke in protest as the outside door slammed and swept open again. The astonished look on Bruce's face was mirrored on his mother's, but the two men seemed neither surprised nor annoyed. After a moment, Elspeth moved, intending either to close the door or follow Hamish, but Andrew stopped her.

"Leave it be, guid wife, and I'll shut the door. Start readin' the next chapter, Bruce!" Glancing at his mother and receiving her nod, Bruce again opened the book.

Reaching the stable, Hamish looked round for some way to vent his feelings. Nellie, the Clydesdale plough horse, sensed his presence and began to stamp nervously. This person could twist a tail or dig into ribs already tender from a day in harness, cruelly hurting in ways that did not show.

In a loud voice Hamish started to ask a few questions about his life. "Just what will happen if I do what I like from now on, instead of what they like?" He answered himself at once. "They could do nothin' to me! Two old men, a woman, and a bit of a lad. They need me more nor I need them. I'm goin' to show them what's what!"

Nellie, her stamping becoming frantic at the sound of the hated voice, nickered in fear. Hamish, forgetful in the excitement of his great discovery, carelessly stepped up behind the horse. Too late he realized his mistake. A massive hoof lashed out, giving him a glancing blow on the shinbone. Gasping with pain, he cursed loudly; then clutching his leg, he hobbled over to where the harness tack hung. Very deliberately choosing a bridle of narrow, plaited leathers, he climbed up onto the wooden boards between the two stalls. Safe now from flashing hooves, Hamish began, very methodically and very brutally, to beat the terrified animal.

Inside the house the reading continued, but this time no one listened. Putting his finger at the place, Bruce stopped again. An uncomfortable silence reigned. Pepper, the old collie, now pensioned off and allowed to spend her time in front of the fire, moved restlessly, emitting a series of low, worried growls. Gran'pa Bruce got up from his place and announced he would go outside to see if the rain had stopped. Young Bruce moved as if to join him, but Andrew's voice halted them both.

"I'll attend to the outside jobs the nicht. It's ower wet and cauld for ye baith. See tae the tea, wife, I willna' be long!" Without so much as a glance at one another, the three went to obey. Andrew seldom used that tone of voice, but when he did, no one demurred. The grandfather banked up the fire before picking up one of the oil lamps and lighting the way for the other two as they passed from the front room to the kitchen. Elspeth had cooked enough stovies on Saturday for both days, and now the good smell, as they warmed in the oven, filled the house.

Opening the oven, she placed a tray of oatcakes beside the brown earthenware dish containing the other food, her thoughts that they always tasted better after a second firing uppermost in her mind. Soon everything was ready, the three seated, waiting for father and son to take their usual places.

Then Andrew or Gran'pa Bruce would ask the blessing, and the meal could begin.

"I wonder what can be takin' them so long?" Elspeth's question was more puzzled than impatient. Both missing men were creatures of habit, and Hamish especially was never late for meals. Bruce looked across at his grandfather before asking, "Gran'pa, should I go and see what's keeping them?" At that precise moment the unmistakable thunder of a gunshot shattered the quiet of the Sunday afternoon.

-·◦⊰{ **5** }⊱◦·-

Young Bruce was the first to reach the stable, closely followed by his grandfather. Elspeth paused only long enough to snatch up a shawl for her head before racing after them. A marrow-chilling sight met her. Too late the old man called out to Bruce, "Keep your mother away 'til I see how bad he is!"

"I'm here already, and I'm stayin', Gran'pa, so don't waste time worryin' about me. Is he breathin'?" Kneeling on the cobblestones, Gran'pa placed his hand over Andrew's chest.

"Och, aye! He's alive, but he's been shot in a bad place. Thank God the pellets couldn't have penetrated either the heart or any other important parts. At least I dinna' think so."

Having heard his grandfather declare that Andrew was alive, young Bruce rushed over to the horses. Nellie was thrashing about her stall in a frenzy. Speaking soothingly, Bruce began to stroke her neck. His hand came away covered with blood. Frantically he cried, "Nellie's been shot, too, her hide is bleedin'!"

"Never mind the horse 'til we see to Andrew. Somebody will have to go to Aribaig for Dr. Black, but first we maun do all we can for him oorsel's."

"We daren't move him, Gran'pa. If anything is broken, it must be set before we even try!"

"Och! Lass we couldna' move him in ony case. Bring yon blanket, an' Bruce, run and fetch another one from the bed.

We'll cover him up and fold one under his heed. Elspeth, you'll bide here with him while Bruce and masel' go to Aribaig for the doctor."

Elspeth shook her head stubbornly. "No, Gran'pa! That's our job. Bruce and I will ride to Aribaig. You must stay with Andrew. Bruce, saddle Nellie, and I'll go for the blanket and a flask of tea as well. We'll be a while!"

"We can't take Nellie, Mam, she's hurt and bleedin' herself, awful bad!" The boy's voice broke in a sob. Never before, in all his twelve years of life, had Bruce experienced anything like what was happening now. Recognizing that the mare had received a cruel beating, he guessed how it came about. He remembered how he often had surprised Hamish tormenting the animals, but this was the worst yet!

"We'll have to take Joshua then. I know he's not broken to the saddle, but he'll just have to get used to it, and in a hurry, too! It would take too long for us to walk."

"Aye, indeed, away in for the blanket, Elspeth, lass, and the tea. Bruce, you hurry now and make up a pail o' mash for baith the horses afore ye go. I'm thinkin' Andrew here is goin' to be fine. In fact if I didn' ken better, I'd say he was just sound asleep and having a guid dream . . ., and look, the color is comin' back into his cheeks." Now that the immediate danger seemed to be passing, the wondering began afresh. How could Andrew have been shot with his own gun lying here on the ground beside him? Where could Hamish be? Should they tell the local constable or keep it to themselves? Elspeth solved the last question as she returned with the blankets. She also brought a tray containing the food from the oven, a bit scorched but still edible.

"No sense Gran'pa starving while he waits and watches. Anyway it would just dry up and be wasted!" Somehow reassured her husband would be all right, she now reverted to her role of caring for their simple needs.

"Dr. Black will know if Constable Graham should be told!" Elspeth spoke the words as she dished out a heaping plate of stovies for each of them. Glancing quickly at Andrew, where he lay supported by the folded blanket and covered with the other one, her words echoed those of Gran'pa.

"He'll do fine I think, now I wonder! . . . Where . . .?"

"Eat some stovies yersel', then be on yer way, lass. Andrew seems fine the now as ye say, but then we canna' be sure."

Joshua stood meekly enough with the unfamiliar saddle and bridle in place. Bruce helped his mother to mount before jumping up behind her. Leaning over, he spoke to his grandfather, his voice intense.

"Gran'pa?"

"Aye, Bruce?"

"Could we not, I mean, should we not pray first? We always talk about layin' hands on folk and prayin' for them to get better, but I've never seen us do it, in the kirk or anywhere else. Even Fraser. . . ." The two adults stared at each other. Elspeth was first to look away. She would allow the old man to answer this one.

"Aye, Brucie, indeed an' you're right. The Lord says to call on Him. He says, 'Ask anything of My Father who is in heaven, and it shall be done if two or three are in agreement.' We'll do it." Struggling to his feet, he reached up to join his hands with the boy's. After only a second's hesitation, Elspeth put one hand in each of theirs.

"Gracious heavenly Father, we're shamed that our prayers become more fervent in desperate need, like the now. Oor deep desire is that we be always in this true communion wi' Yersel', but Lord, You made us, an' You ken us weel. Forgive and love us just the same. Thank Ye, Lord! Oor petition is for the man Andrew Cormack here. According to your Book, Lord, we take dominion ower whatever it is that is attacking this body of your child Andrew. We demand that it leave now in the name of Jesus, that the empty spaces be filled wi' peace. Gie us wisdom, Lord, and help us to help him. Return his good health and strength as Ye promise to make us a' 'every whit whole.' In Jesus' name, amen."

Some days later Bruce picked up the plaited leather strapping caked with dried blood. He said nothing as he handed the damning evidence to his grandfather. Hamish Cormack had disappeared, and no one pretended to be sorry. Still Bruce could not shake the feeling that all was not at an end between him and his stepbrother.

Meanwhile, Bruce never forgot the story of Andrew's experience the day he fell over supposedly shot dead, which he wrote at his stepfather's dictation.

"It's a sad thing, son, but you willna' be able to tell this to ower many. The Lord Hissel' will show ye the ones to be told, but we mauna cast pearls before swine, as the Scripture itsel' says, and a revelation like this is indeed a 'pearl of great price'! Happy as I am to bide here with yer mother and yersel', now that I've had a taste of the ither side, I'm afraid I'm impatient to go on." Listening, Bruce also became a bit impatient, not to go on, but to hear the rest of the story.

"Tell me, what was it like, Father?" he said now.

"Aye, I'll tell ye when the others come ben; then it'll be the one telling. You can write it a' doon so that we don't forget or try to change any of it!" Elspeth walked into the room as he finished speaking, closely followed by Gran'pa. Although they both had other matters pulling at their thoughts, this day neither had any intention of missing Andrew's testimony. All was in readiness, and the sense of drama heightened as young Bruce waited, his sharpened pencil held aloft over the ream of snow-white foolscap his mother had produced from the kist. Along with the expectancy, or rather merged with it, there was a feeling of reverent awe.

"First I want to tell you about the peacefulness; it was past description, past understanding, truly as the Bible says." Something else was happening, but now only one of the listeners seemed aware of it. Andrew's voice had assumed a different style of speaking. His words came forth as the words of the learned, completely unknown to have been his vocabulary before.

"Seeing as there is no time at all in Kingdom living, then that must be the reason I felt no need to hurry up for anything. I only had to think of something, and it already happened. Like I was not arguing or asking for answers. I merely thought of it, and the answer appeared ready in my mind. I do not recall any one thing, but I did think, *If this keeps up, I'll be able to read and write in no time.* Sure enough the thought brought the answer, *If I'm to stay here a while longer, I pray the ability to read and write will stay with me!*" Andrew stopped speaking to rest, and the smile on his face could only be described as beatific. His audience of three stared at one another, and Bruce had stopped writing some minutes ago. Never before had Andrew Cormack spoken so many words at once. In fact his sentences were usually short to the point of brusqueness. Today however, he spoke words that before this he would not have known how to say, let alone known their meaning.

Andrew continued into the awed silence. "I felt no pain, no ache, only complete comfort and joy. Before that happened, though, I had gone through a stage of wondering how to conduct myself with Hamish. I would not be able to hurt him in any way of retaliation, I knew that, but my feelings of anger, when I saw what he was doing to Nellie, were murderous. Frightfully so! Therefore I died in a way even before the shot hit me. While I was crying out to God for wisdom, at the same time I asked Him to forgive my murderous thoughts. The burning sensation as I fell to the ground lasted only a moment. Immediately I was standing on a lovely beach. The sea was of glass but only because there was no wind to disturb it, and as I went to walk on it I realized instantly why I could. I weighed nothing at all! The law of gravity, as it operates here on the earth, was not needed there. The whole theory of gravity was revealed to me as I thought of it, and it came as no surprise.

"Then I saw the gates of pearl, not in solid form, but two beautiful, milky white clouds, each one a perfect, translucent column. Yet they had nothing of coldness or wetness as clouds of mist are here. As I started to walk through, they appeared to unfold before me; but before I got too far, a voice sounded in my thoughts. *Andrew, Andrew, I have more for you to do on the earth yet, and you must tell Bruce and the boy, as well as your wife, all that I allow to remain in your memory when you return to them.* Knowing that this indeed was the Lord speaking, I dared not question, so here I am. One more thing I must say to you. I was in Paradise with Jesus for a little while. I'll be going there again someday, and so will you three. While I was there, I learned many things, but I don't believe I will be allowed to remember them all. This is best, because I will only pine to go there again. I also know I will be allowed to keep some of my learning, like reading, writing, arithmetic, and some of the ideas of how machines work. We are not to tell of all this yet, but we may make a record of it, and sometime, somebody will be allowed to tell it. I'm finished now, and I'm going to sleep for a while." Saying this, Andrew leaned back on his pillow and closed his eyes. No one else moved. His three listeners sat on, still very much in silent awe. Then Bruce, on a signal from his mother, resumed his writing.

Gran'pa had closed his eyes, but he was far from sleep. Never had he doubted the Bible messages, since first hearing them from his Band of Hope leaders long long ago. But the things he was hearing today, he knew, they could not share with any but themselves. Suddenly he got down on his knees beside the chair. At the same moment his grandson, also feeling the reverence, put down the writing as he, too, fell on his knees. Elspeth, tears streaming down her face, knelt with them. Bruce broke the silence at last.

'In Thy presence, Lord, is indeed fullness of joy!" A hearty amen echoed from the others in the room.

6

Bruce wondered why he bothered to stand gazing out of his attic window. For one thing the sloped ceiling, or "coomb ceilin'," as his grandfather called it, where the window was set, made it awkward and painful for his six-foot frame to fit. If he folded himself over backward, trying to see out, he got an immediate crick in his neck. If he tried to look forward, he received the distinct feeling that his eyes would remain permanently fixed to the top lids, leaving only the whites to stare blankly at the view. Today he could say, "And what view?" It being no more than a hazy curtain of gray drizzle, the same as it had been for the last five days. No hills in the background, no farm steading in the foreground, not even the ghostly outline of a fence or dirt path would dispel the impression of some remote dream world. Giving up the futility of trying to see out, he withdrew from the opening, only to crack his head sharply as he had done so many times before. He hardly felt the pain, but the noise of the impact penetrated through the open trap door, to where his mother waited below.

"Bruce, are you at it again? Come on down, and I'll give ye something more useful to do than watch the rain fall!"

"Just a minute, Mother!"

Impatience and frustration found their way into his otherwise mild statement, giving Elspeth another proof of the anger she had watched build up in her beloved son this past while. After the episode in which Andrew had touched death and beyond, things at the farm had seemed to move along in a lighter fashion. Of course Hamish had not been seen since that day, and even if this had meant a heavier work load for the others, not a word of complaint passed anyone's lips—at least not until the past few months, and then it could not be said to be complaining exactly.

Elspeth sighed. She could not put her finger on it. Likely Gran'pa was right, and she didn't want to let go of Bruce. Let go she must though, as her own dream for him could not come about unless he went away. At the moment, even if she felt angry at him, stuck up in his attic room and obviously discontented, she tried to be fair as she thought back to when this all began. It seemed that suddenly the village school became too tight to hold Bruce. He questioned his stepfather and even his grandfather, sometimes only with a dark look so foreign to his usually bright features. Other times he merely shrugged his shoulders or, more often in recent weeks, simply rose from the table and left the room as Andrew or Gran'pa mentioned the things of God. Yes, and it all stemmed from the time when their family friend and Bruce's teacher, Reverend Fraser Clegg, left the school and subsequently the parish to answer a call to the mission field. Leaving the tangled skein of her thoughts as Bruce clattered down the stairs, she smiled. One thing was certain; the lad was going to the university, and very soon—this week in fact. In two more days he would board the train at Fort William and be off to the big city—not Edinburgh, but Glasgow.

"It's all right, son, there's nothing that pressin' it can't wait until ye're ready!" Immediately she was rewarded by his smile before he turned to go back up the stairs.

"Thanks, Mother, there is something else I want to do. Then I'll be down."

What Bruce had to do was something he had been postponing for a long time—ever since his friend Fraser had left Aribaig in fact. Not exactly sure when it had started, he recognized that he had been finding it more and more difficult to pray. There were times, so frequent now that they could no longer be ignored, when he wanted to deny everything he had ever learned about God. A shiver ran through his body as he at last allowed himself to confront this fact. He groaned softly, knowing that also to be a form of prayer.

"Oh! If only I could empty myself of all I've learned and had put into me from Mother, Andrew, Fraser, and yes, even Gran'pa. I want a chance to start again and learn for myself, firsthand, looking on from the outside for a while and then making my own decision—not having to please any but me." The age-old cry was coming from deep within, and young as he was, Bruce realized this could only be spirit reaching out to Spirit. The very thing his mother drew comfort from, his ingrown knowledge of the Bible through memory verses, was now causing him this agony. "Why art thou cast down, O my soul? and why art thou disquieted in me? hope thou in God. . . ." *Disquieted indeed! I can be asking myself all these questions or asking God, whom I'm not even sure exists anymore.* As if in answer, his mind echoed, *Yes, deep calleth unto deep!* Getting up from where he had been sitting, on top of his cot, Bruce shook himself, smiling ruefully as he did so. "It is really quite funny, if I didn't feel so hellish!" Their newest collie, named Spicer, had only today at dinnertime made them all laugh as he shook himself, exactly as Bruce had just done, to get rid of the water drenching his thick coat, showering Bruce at the same time.

"I'm just like Spicer, trying to get rid of whatever it is I'm saturated with. Only this won't shake off so easily!" Leaning forward, he brought both hands up to his head, clasping them together at the back, leaving his hair standing on end—a custom reminiscent of his other grandfather, did he but know it.

Still speaking softly to himself, he made his way again to the attic steps, "I must get this sorted out in my mind today, and there is no one to ask. They are all so sure. I would say even *smug,* if I did not love them all so much!" The new dominie who had taken Fraser Clegg's place at the village school was not a believer. He spoke of being of the "New Thought," a Darwinist. This was all part of Bruce's conflict. He liked the man. But even his other grandfather, whom he remembered vaguely with a sinking feeling of fear and somehow shame, was still a believer. Everyone in the village of Aribaig, in fact everyone Bruce had ever known, except this man, was a believer. Until Bouregarde Gallagher (he made jokes about his name, too) came to the school at Aribaig, Bruce had never met anyone who was not a believer. Of course he was the only person in the town who knew this fact. He remembered the day he made the discovery. The figure confronting the assembled school on that first Monday morning after Fraser's departure appeared innocent enough. Bruce, being the oldest pupil, had the responsibility of teaching the beginner's class. Boys and girls, they ranged in age from four years to eleven, depending upon how soon their parents had other children coming along to help with the farm work, and Bruce knew there were many others who would never get to school at all. Be that as it may, he was teaching the infant's class on the Friday of that first week of Mr. Gallagher's reign, reading aloud to them from the Book of Genesis, in the first chapter: "So God created man in his own image, in the image of God he created him, male and female created he them." Suddenly aware of being watched, Bruce stopped speaking and glanced up to find the dominie standing over him with what could only be described as a sneer on his elegantly handsome face. Thinking about it now, in the privacy of his room, Bruce still cringed with embarrassment. Even on such short acquaintance there had sprung up between the two a comradeliness different entirely from that shared with Fraser or any of the other significant men in the inner circle of his life. Later that day, when the children had gone running, clattering and chattering as children do, even if home meant two or three hours of hard work before their dinnertime, Bruce lingered, supposedly cleaning up slates and the blackboards, but really waiting to find out what the new teacher meant by the funny looks he had been throwing about.

Bouregarde Gallagher's mother had been a snob. A romantic but still a snob. Never having the purse to match her ambitions, she had made the most of what she did have: good looks and a vivid imagination. If Bruce MacAlister was unhappy because his whole being had been saturated from birth with things spiritual, then Bouregarde Gallagher could say the same thing, only it was the opposite spirit that his being became saturated with. From early childhood the impressionable Bouregarde watched keenly while his mother plied her trade in the darkened front room in what constituted the Gallagher's portion of a four-dwelling brownstone tenement that had seen better days as a mansion house. Her business was fortune-telling and card and teacup reading; they even had a crystal ball. As he grew older Bouregarde was allowed to assist in setting the scenes for the fakery and deception that went on each time a paying visitor came. That bothered him not at all, and he soon became adept. What he really liked best were the séances. Most of their living came from them, and they also provided the funds for his education. But it interested him mostly because he had discovered it was not all fake! Helping his mother in her preparations, setting curtains just so, and arranging doors so they would open strategically at the correct moment had made him very cynical and contemptuous of the customers, until the day a voice spoke to him. This voice was not part of the plan, and Bouregarde knew instinctively he had never heard a human voice quite like it. From that day on, Bouregarde had played to a different audience and marched to a secret drumbeat, a beat that began to dominate his life and that no one else knew about, not even his mother.

He recognized in Bruce MacAlister a sterling quality of character fused with a kind of vulnerable generosity. In that first confrontation one was just as confounded as the other, each never having experienced such a personality before. The fact that the dominie was not a believer was obviously not common knowledge in the village, or he would not have been given the post. He, being well trained in deception and duplicity, had no trouble concealing his inner thoughts and motives, until he came up against Bruce MacAlister. Swishing the rag once more across an already spotless blackboard, the youth waited. He had been taught never to speak until spoken to within the confines of school and church, and this tradition had been adhered to even with his friend Fraser. So now he waited.

At last it came: "We will dispense with filling their heads with all that mythical Judeo-Christian teaching, Mr. MacAlister. While I am teacher here, this book will remain closed and inside the desk!" Picking up the Bible as he spoke, the dominie closed it with a snap before dropping it into the recess of the desk. Bruce made no comment, but he still did not move.

"Well! What have you to say? You may speak. I have formed the opinion that, as you stand out from the others here, you must be that rare being, a person who can never get enough of learning. So you must always have questions. Don't be afraid to ask them."

"My first and only question is this, 'How can you be a teacher if you believe the Bible is mythical?' "

For a moment of shocked silence Bruce thought Mr. Gallagher would strike him, but all at once he began to laugh instead. Then suddenly the laughter came to an abrupt stop.

"It is not general knowledge that I don't believe the Bible, and you won't tell anyone, because if you do, and I lose this job, I'll kill you!" The black eyes flashed fire, but fire with no warmth. The whole encounter had taken only a very few minutes, and as Bruce turned, shivering, away from the chilling look, it disappeared from the teacher's face as if it had never been. When he spoke again, his voice resumed the cool nonchalance of the past week, yet the words still held their note of warning for Bruce.

"Now that we understand each other, maybe we can get acquainted and become friends." In spite of himself, almost without the consent of his will, Bruce found he was being drawn into a relationship completely outside anything he had ever experienced before. It had culminated in his present dilemma.

Standing by the kitchen window, directly under the attic where her son was having the conflict, Elspeth contemplated the same outlook of rain and cloud. As usual in her rare moments of inactivity, she prayed.

"O Lord! Please let the rain stop long enough to dry up the roads in time for Friday's coach to get through to the train." Even as she prayed, something they had not seen in six days caught her eye. It was so surprising that she didn't at first believe the evidence of her senses. Then as she looked again her spirits began to rise, and she continued to pray. "We of little faith, Lord. You know us so well. I dare to believe my prayer is being answered." She remembered the Bible verse describing how Elisha's servant, Caleb, having been sent to test the sky for rain clouds, had at first not believed his sight either, but on looking for a second time he perceived a cloud the size of a man's fist. This could be the same thing only in reverse. She saw a break in the clouds, a tiny speck of blue sky. Almost tearful in her joy, she held up a small, work-worn fist to measure the bright space. Yes, indeed! "It's the size of a woman's fist!" Her excited cry echoed through the silent house and brought responses from every region. First Spicer started barking furiously; then Bruce came bounding down the stairs, almost but not quite his old self again. From the direction of the front room, where they had been praying a very different petition from Elspeth's, walked the other two members of the household.

The break in the clouds swelled and grew larger, reminding the watchers of the curtain parting on the stage of the village hall when they attended concerts there. Suddenly this impression became more enhanced by the unexpected appearance of a small, black figure, seeming to walk up center stage. Within moments the figure was close enough for the audience to recognize him. No one spoke, each busy with his or her own interpretation of the reason for this visitation, and none wished to break the silence. Spicer had no such niceties built in him. On first sensing the stranger, his hackles rose alarmingly, charged by the instinctive current of his ingrained foretaste of doom.

The growl, beginning deep in the animal's throat, emerged as a full-fledged howling. Still fulfilling instinct, the dog pointed his muzzle skyward; setting up such a cry, he seemed quite prepared to keep up for as long as he deemed it necessary. Spicer recognized a foe, and no amount of coaxing or kind words would convince him otherwise.

It took the combined efforts of Bruce and his grandfather to hold the dog back as the visitor advanced. Then as Elspeth, with something of her normal courteous manners lacking, reluctantly held open the front door, thereby inviting Dominie Gallagher to enter, the men half carried, half dragged the still-howling dog to the cartshed, where they chained him thoroughly to the heaviest cart. Spicer tried feverishly to free himself, but on finding it futile, he settled down with a dismal whine of protest that, although it set Bruce's teeth on edge, also had the effect of making him want to weep.

Pushing aside these foolish thoughts, he said, "Come on, Gran'pa, Mr. Gallagher will think we're a clique o' uncivilized country yokels. I'm fair ashamed o' that dog!"

"Dinna be ower hard on Spicer, Brucie. He's only doin' what his instincts tell him, an' I masel' canna blame the beast. The dominie's eyes make me feel uneasy as well."

"Oh, Gran'pa, I'm surprised at you. The teacher is a well-educated gentleman, and we should be honored he's visiting us!" Bruce the elder looked long and deep at his grandson, and it was the latter who first dragged his eyes away, turning to run into the house. The grandfather followed very slowly.

$\cdot\cdot\circ\cdot\{7\}\cdot\circ\cdot$

Elspeth was flustered.

"I'll make some tea, Mr. Gallagher, and you'll take a scone. They're hot off the griddle and. . . ." Unlike herself, she tried to hide her lack of ease and her anxiety with many words. Her relief was evident when Bruce entered the kitchen, with Gran'pa close behind him.

"Did you settle that dog? I can't think what came over him. He's never. . . ."

"It's all right, Mrs. Cormack. I won't have any tea, thank you just the same. I came to bring Bruce a small '*bon voyage*' gift, and then I must be off, as I promised to have the horse back to town before dark. What weather! I'm thankful for my oilskin cape and cap." As he spoke the visitor handed Bruce a package, unmistakably a book, wrapped in thick brown paper and covered on the outside with a piece of transparent oiled silk. "Good luck, my young friend, and '*au 'voir!*' " Before Bruce could gather himself together enough to so much as thank him, he had lifted the latch and disappeared into the lingering mists.

Andrew, a silent onlooker to all this, had not moved from his chair during the whole encounter. It had taken only a matter of fifteen or twenty minutes by the wall clock, but so much had transpired. In the meantime the four people in the room appeared stunned.

At last Andrew spoke, his words leaving no doubt about his

feelings: "Bruce, lad, your visitor is a son of perdition, and his gift is a curse. Throw it on the fire before it blights your life!" Bruce looked round the anxious, loving faces in the room. Agreement with Andrew was written all too plainly on each one.

"No! No! No! Are we all going daft, to let a dog dictate what we'll do? I will not burn my gift. It was given me in good faith, out of kindness, and I'll accept it the same way. What he must think of us I dread to imagine. A bunch of dolts, standing with our mouths hanging open, being influenced by a great lump of a dog!" Bruce left them then, and pushing past his mother, who was by now crying quietly, he ran back up to his attic room. The silence he left behind was so thick you could almost see it. Elspeth at last broke it. "The dog's stopped!"

"I'll go and get him. He'll be all right now that—" Gran'pa did not finish the sentence but left the room quickly.

"Wife, dinna greet! The lad'll be fine. You'll see. I made it worse by suggestin' he burn the book. It could only be a book, and I would guess no' the Bible. Our lad has sense, and I believe he'll burn it hissel, o' his own accord, and aye before he goes awa' to Glasgow. Now what aboot the tea? The scones smell good." At once Elspeth turned to the fireplace, and as she swung the kettle round on its hook, to dangle over the heart of the flames, Gran'pa reentered the room, a very subdued Spicer at his heels. Too subdued, the usually buoyant animal slunk to a corner, his tail curled up between his legs, and the people in the room stared at him unbelievingly, before sharing bewildered looks with each other. *Whatever now?* the looks seemed to say.

Walking over to the pantry, Elspeth said, "I'll get him a bit meat, that'll cheer him up!" but she was wrong. Nothing would entice Spicer. Not even when a shamefaced Bruce came downstairs and leaned down to pat him, would the dog respond beyond a desultory lick of Bruce's hand. After a while they gave up. The mealtime and the remainder of the evening passed quietly.

On his way to lock up for the night, Andrew said, "He'll be his ain' self in the mornin', you'll see!"

In this he, too, was wrong. When the family came together in the morning, Spicer lay in his corner, on the old mat that was exclusively his bed, exactly the way they had left him the night before, with one difference. Bruce reached the bottom stair in time to hear his mother's shocked gasp.

Elspeth had arisen at her usual hour, and walking over to start the fire to make breakfast, she bent over to pat the dog before letting him run outside. *Spicer is lying in an odd position,* she thought. Her cry brought the others running, but unlike the day before, this cry was filled with horror and disbelief.

"Oh, my word! Andrew, Bruce, come here, what—?"

"It's some kind of curse, put on an innocent animal. But we can and will stand against the evil one. In the name of Jesus we come against you, Satan and your hordes. We rebuke your curse, and we claim the protection of the blood of Jesus upon this place and all who dwell here!" Bruce was holding his mother as all her pent-up fears and frustrations came to a head. She sobbed it out in a way she never had before. The dead dog had been the final straw. The old man was turning Spicer over as he examined him to see if there was a reason, beyond what Andrew had just decreed, for the sudden death. He found nothing.

An hour later, as the four of them sat round the breakfast table, not able to eat but drinking the pot of hot, strong tea, so needed and helpful in a crisis, the head of the family spoke again: "This is a' a great pity about the dog, but it has the good effect of showin' up the dominie. The gift of discernment of the spirit of evil is not a happy gift at the time, but once it has been put to use, it always works out for the best. God wants us to discern evil so that we can resist and flee from it. Bruce, do not fear the Mr. Gallaghers, for '. . . greater is he that is in you, than he that is in the world.' That means the Holy Spirit, who indwells Bruce MacAlister, is greater than the spirit of anti-christ, who dwells within the dominie. I'm sorry, lad, but we must face the truth. Now we will pray for his eternal soul. Christ wants none to perish, but when yon dominie declared that he willed not to believe in Jesus, he was blaspheming the work of the Holy Spirit. That is the unforgivable sin. However, only God can judge, and we still must pray for him."

"What else should we do, Father?" Bruce, no longer doubting, as only God could have revealed all this to his stepfather, wondered if he now should report to the education authorities what he knew about Mr. Bouregarde Gallagher.

"Nothing else, son. We will all just carry on, and you will continue your preparation to go to Glasgow. I have the strong notion that God will look after it all, even the school. Would you all not agree on that?"

"Aye. Amen!"

"Yes!" and another "amen" were hearty confirmation of that agreement as each one hurried off to belated morning duties, having not only the two lost hours to make up, but a week of rain and, for Bruce, many months of questioning and rebellion.

It was ten o'clock precisely on the wall clock. A brilliant sun climbed high in a clear blue sky when Dugald the Postie brought the news.

"Aye! He must have fell off the horse when it slipped on the wet bridge. The burn was high wi' a' the rain, but the body didna' go faur! They fished him oot aboot hauf a mile from the toon. His long, waterproof cape taigled up his arms and legs enough tae keep him from swimmin' for it. Aye! weel, such is life. In the midst of it we are in death, as the guid book says. Thankfu' we are in the toon that Geordie's horse is nane the worse for it." Speechless, Elspeth poured the ever-ready cup of tea for the postman, waiting for further comments, but Dugald was finished with that subject. He did not need to name the flood victim. All four of his listeners knew. Pausing in the act of devouring a scone liberally spread with strawberry jam, Dugald turned toward the three men standing in the doorway.

"Twa letters for Brucie. My he's an important man nooadays! Awa' tae the university is it? Well I must get on ma way. Thank ye for the tea, mistress."

Dugald the Post was well on his way and the family seated for a late dinner. Gran'pa Bruce had the Bible open on the table in front of him. Andrew had asked for a special reading before blessing the food.

"He suffered no man to do them wrong: yea, he reproved kings for their sakes; saying touch not mine anointed, and do my prophets no harm."

His eyes moving to the fire as his grandfather read a familiar passage from the book of 1 Chronicles, Bruce watched the flames lick round the leather covers of a book after they had devoured its paper wrappings. Clearly, for a last moment before disappearing in a shower of sparks, the gold letters of the title and author on the book's spine stood out: *Origin of the Species*, by *Charles Darwin*. Bruce would read that book and be in many debates about its contents later, as part of his studies in Christian apologetics, but by then he would also be more fully equipped for the battle.

8

As his train puffed its way into Glasgow's Central Station a great flood of emotion swept through Bruce MacAlister. Mixed in with the excitement and thrill of the new adventure unfolding before him came the relief that at last he was here, in this fabled city, about to discover *life!*

Walking the short distance to George Street, Bruce stopped to gaze in awestruck wonder at the tall columns of the statues, resolving to come back soon to study the names more closely. Finding a summer seat, he carefully laid down his bundle before taking the small notebook from his pocket once more to confirm the address of the place as Strathcona House, on George Street. He leaned back with a sigh of happy anticipation, silently thanking Fraser for providing them with the landlady's name. Fraser himself had stayed here, twenty years ago, when he attended Glasgow University. Bruce jumped to his feet and picked up his bundle. Strathcona House must be just round the corner.

Fifteen minutes later he strode smartly up a set of neat sandstone steps leading to a most impressive teak door. From his reading he guessed the door was from India as was the bright brass doorbell dazzling his eyes as it caught the early morning sun. Bruce reached over to pull it down. A sound, patterned on Big Ben itself, did Bruce but know it, jangled deep in the recesses of the building; and after what seemed an endless time, the door opened to reveal a small woman, dressed in a maid's cap and apron, framed in the arched space.

"Yes?"

Trying to hide his discomfort, Bruce said, "Mrs. MacIntyre, please!"

"Are you Mr. MacAlister?"

"Yes, I am."

"Well, you can come in this time, and I'll show you your room, but in the future use the side door. Mrs. MacIntyre will not see you before dinnertime, when she her own self will serve the dinner to all the new students." Feeling rather as if he should somehow acknowledge this honor, Bruce followed the diminutive servant up one flight of stairs before she turned along a large open balcony. Then she led him through to a narrower, steeper, flight of stairs, and Bruce found himself praying his room would not have an attic ceiling. In his close to nineteen years, this first time away from home alone would create its own nostalgia if he were to be lodged in a room like his own at the croft. The thought of that familiar, cozy place started up a fresh wave of loneliness, but not for long. The maid stopped at a door, but before she could open it, a voice came from behind them.

"Betsy!" Turning to view this new arrival, Bruce watched as first a curly red head, followed by a neatly crinolined form appeared at the top of the narrow stairwell.

"Betsy!" Bruce's guide faced the owner of the voice.

"Yes, Miss Jean?"

"Granny wants you. I'm to show the new students to their rooms—"

"But Miss Jean. She said—"

"Granny's waiting for you, Betsy, you'd better hurry up!" Betsy hurried away along the narrow upper hallway, squeezing past the young woman she had addressed as Miss Jean. The two persons left on the narrow, ledgelike balcony simply gazed at each other. Then Bruce, realizing he must be gawking, glanced away. Girls like this were out of his experience entirely.

At home in Aribaig, even at the school, girls usually stayed in their places until the bell rang, then ran off to the farms and the jobs always waiting. By age eleven or twelve most of the girls left school to go into service or help their mothers, thereby making room for younger brothers and sisters coming up. Whatever the reason for it, in the words of his gran'pa, he was "fair flummoxed."

Jean Irvine, for her part, was almost as bad. Although she had seen many students during the years, this one seemed to be having quite a strange effect on her. Calling together her wandering thoughts, she spoke at last: "I'm Jean Irvine. Mrs. MacIntyre is my grandmother. I believe you are Mr. MacAlister?"

Staring at what he considered to be the most beautiful creature he had ever seen, Bruce's tongue failed him.

Moments passed, and then the vision spoke again. "If you are Mr. MacAlister, this is your room, but if you are Mr. Blair, then your room is farther along the lobby!" The pink color creeping up Bruce's neck turned to a fiery red as he finally managed to blurt out, "Oh, no! I mean yes. MacAlister." His voice choked on his name, making it sound just like that time when he had to stop singing in the choir. But at least now she knew he could speak.

"Granny insists that everyone, family and student boarders alike, be on time for meals. She is very strict about it. She also has rules about bedmaking and tidy rooms. No sleeping in, except on Saturday and Sunday, when breakfast is at eight o'clock, rather than a quarter to seven." It was her turn to blush as Jean Irvine realized the intimacies of talking to a strange young man on the threshold of his bedroom.

Backing slowly in the direction of the stairs, she continued to speak to the still-silent Bruce: "Dinner is at twelve o'clock sharp then. Granny will explain the house rules at that time." She vanished down the narrow staircase.

Echoing in Bruce's head above all the things she had said was this: Family and student boarders were expected to be on time for meals. If that meant what he thought it meant, he would be seeing this lovely, red-haired vision often—maybe even every day and most definitely today at dinnertime. His homesickness left, to be quickly replaced by self-doubts. A lot of good it would be to see her every day, just to stand and gawk at her like a sick calf. Bruce wondered if it was lawful to pray for courage at a time like this and decided to try it anyway. Slowly he pushed open the door into what was to become his private haven for the next four years; he heaved his bundle onto the snowy coverlet, and still in a dreamlike state, he knelt beside the bed to talk things over with God in prayer.

The clock on his bedside table registered twenty minutes to twelve, and Bruce waited impatiently for the big hand to meet the small one. Following his session of prayer he felt much calmer and confident he would be able to deal with anything. Finding a basin of water and a towel, he splashed his face before opening up his bundle to get his best shirt. Carefully he placed his other clothes in the chest of drawers under the one small window. The room was not very big, but at least he would have it to himself, and he could stand up straight anywhere in the room, without bumping his head. The walls, although close together, were equal in height, allowing him space to walk upright all the time. Bruce glanced at the clock again. The thing must be stopped. He removed the brand-new pocket watch, Gran'pa's gift, bestowed upon him yesterday as they all stood together on the station platform, noting that indeed only one minute had elapsed since he had last looked. Then he heard heavy footsteps, which stopped outside his door. Rising to his feet, Bruce waited for he knew not what. As the door was thrust inward, there, facing Bruce, stood one of the largest young men he had ever seen, and he had seen many!

"Hello, I'm Peter Blair. You must be Bruce MacAlister? I took the liberty of asking the maid, Betsy, I believe, what your name might be. A most obliging girl."

Finding his hand enveloped in a massive but surprisingly

gentle clasp, he replied, "Yes, I am Bruce MacAlister. Pleased to meet you!"

"Oh, you speak English then? and very well, if I may say so."

"I hope I do. It's my native tongue, although I have the Gaelic as well. I intend to master the Latin, Greek, etcetera, after I've been a while doing what I came here to do at the university!"

"Touché! It's a 'cute one as well, is it?"

"It seems to be just on the dinner hour. Could you tell me what you wanted, and I'll be on my way to the dining room."

"Oh, I'll go with you. I only wanted to see what you were like. I'm satisfied we'll get on fine together, and we can get even better acquainted this afternoon. But first, let us hie to the culinary center, as the smell is fair ticklin' ma juices till I'm almost drooned in them. Do you like to curl or hike? I'm daft on both, hikin' in summer and curlin' in winter, or maybe you're a lawn booler, or what about golf?" Bruce continued to shake his head, amazed at the speed of his new companion's questions. Breathless, they reached the bottom of the second set of stairs just as Betsy stood ready in front of the table, holding a formidable brass gong. Like the teak door, it had the look of the East about it, but it was not there for decoration as they soon discovered. Betsy had a mallet poised, and now as the two lads walked across the hall, the boom reverberated throughout the entire household. It would become an integral part of the pattern of their life for four years. For the moment, though, even Peter Blair was startled out of his natural aplomb. Bruce seated himself at his place at the table—no mistaking that, because his name was printed out very neatly on a white card in front of him. He smiled faintly. *I'll like it fine here*, he thought as Betsy filled his soup bowl from the big tureen in the middle of the table. But had he judged too soon? He still had to meet Granny!

It was Mrs. Beulah MacIntyre's custom to bring out everything about everyone residing or about to reside in her home at their first meal together. This formal inquisition was due to begin the very minute the main course was cleared away and the tea with "afters" served. An elegant, silver-spined, three-tiered plate now graced the exact spot where the tureen had earlier reigned supreme. Bruce resolved to measure it sometime. Upon this plate rested such a variety of fancy cakes that Bruce knew he would never be able to make up his mind which to choose. Thinking about this and wondering if he should risk reaching out for one of those sumptuous looking cream buns, his hand was arrested in midair as he heard his name.

"Mr. MacAlister, would you be so kind as to tell us why you chose to take up the study of theology?"

Completely taken aback, he found himself stuttering again, "Why, ma'am, I don't! It was chust, I mean I want to preach the Gospel!"

"I understand that, but why?"

"Well, because it was our Lord's great commission."

"I know that, too, and you know it, yet of the two of us you are the one to take it up. Know ye why?"

"It must be that I recognize the call, and I accept the challenge! Ma'am."

There was a moment of silence, then, "Please call me Mrs. MacIntyre."

Jean, who had been holding her breath as she toyed with a piece of cake on her plate, breaking it into little bits and pressing them together again, gave a tiny sigh of relief before popping the much-abused pastry into her mouth. He had passed.

Granny spoke again, "You are the son of a croft farmer, and your mother, who writes an excellent letter, tells me that you are a very steady fellow, having made good marks in school, winning a bursary and tutoring young children to earn your own university entrance." Mrs. MacIntyre was saying this for the purpose of introduction, a statement, not a question. Bruce groaned inwardly, wondering what else his mother had told this auspicious lady. She went on, "Extremely commendable I'm sure, and a mother could write no less about her own. However, we'll see, time will tell! Now Mr. Blair, no need to ask you why you wish to become a physician. It's plain for all to see. Just tell me why you wished to stay with us here at Strathcona House? Why did you leave your last place?" The astute landlady's purpose was to introduce, and having her houseguests tell their stories within hearing of each other as well as the family and servants saved idle gossip and stopped foolish guessing. The normally garrulous Peter was silent. *Should I bluff it*, he thought, *or could she possibly know already?* Deciding to risk all for truth, he blurted, "I was asked not to come back to my last lodgings, Mrs. MacIntyre, ma'am!"

"Oh, indeed, and can you tell us why?"

"It was all due to Penelope."

"Aha! Penelope?"

"She was my white mouse, and I had her for the experiments. They did not come out right, and I grew real fond of the cratur', but one day she got out of her cage and found her way to Mrs. Crawford's own bedroom."

"Say no more, Mr. Blair. I can fully sympathize with your Mrs. Crawford. But pray, where now is Penelope?"

"I left her at home in Burntisland. My wee brother is takin' care of her for me."

"Good, we wouldn't want such an occurrence to be repeated." Bruce dared a glance up from his plate to see if he was right in fancying he detected a faint tremor in the old lady's voice, but her face remained poker straight as she passed to the next introductions.

"Mr. MacAlister, on your right is Mr. Davidson, and on his right is Mr. Leekie. Both these gentlemen are with us for the third year, and Mr. D. is also in theology, while Mr. L. is in medicine. No doubt you will all have much to discuss among yourselves. Meanwhile here are the conditions upon which we run our establishment." The rest of the speech flowed over Bruce and sounded ordinary enough. It should prove easy to comply with. No late hours, no strong drink, rent and board money to be paid promptly in advance. No visitors in bedrooms. All very commonplace until, ". . . And now we will talk about Jean, my granddaughter here. With four young men in the house, not of our family, it must be said at the outset that Jean is not allowed to be alone with any of you at any time. She may converse with you while I am in the room or with Betsy present, but there is no other exception to this rule. Now gentlemen, I believe we understand one another." Jean squirmed in her seat as her grandmother continued, "As you are aware, I am Mrs. MacIntyre, a minister's widow, and I take in student boarders for three reasons. The first one is financial; the small return enables me to remain under my own roof. Another is that I do enjoy having younger folks about me. My third and to me most-important reason is that I am a Christian believer, and I endeavor to bring those living in my home into a deeper knowledge of Jesus Christ. Daily Bible readings and prayers, in addition to table grace, are part of life at Strathcona House. If this should prove objectionable to anyone here, then of course you are free to leave us. Good day to you. Tea will be served promptly at half past five o'clock. . . . Jean!"

The girl rose from the table and walked to her grandmother's side. The two left the room together. Betsy, waiting just inside the door, moved quickly to the table. The two senior students, still having said not a word between them, left the room after stacking their dirty dishes on the trolley next to the sideboard. Peter quickly followed suit, and Bruce, catching the obvious, added his dishes to the pile. The maid finished clearing up and left, too, pushing the trolley ahead of her.

"Whew!" It was more of an explosion than a word, and Peter looked in Bruce's direction. Suddenly they began softly to laugh. The pent-up emotion of the past weeks and now the experiences of the morning simply took their toll on Bruce. The vision of a wee white mouse harmlessly occupying the never-met landlady's bed was too much. Peter Blair, his huge body shaking with mirth, was in agony, trying to remain silent, but it was no use. Another explosion shook his frame; this time he laughed out loud.

"Penelope!" and they were off again, holding onto each other helplessly.

"May I ask what is so highly amusing, or is it a men-only joke?" Instantly sober, the two watched now as the beautiful redhead moved round to the chair so recently vacated by her grandmother, picking up the fringed black shawl she had been sent to retrieve. Stopping at the door, she turned.

"Betsy and I take a walk in the square at three o'clock of an afternoon. We usually sit under Sir Walter's statue, on the summer seat!" Quickly she turned her eyes from Bruce before hurrying off with the shawl.

Sir Walter's statue towered disdainfully, dwarfing other, lesser memorials surrounding the famous square. The two young women, seated demurely under it, taking the air so innocently, watched Bruce and Peter approaching. Bruce would much rather have been by himself, but Peter could not be shaken off.

"You are goin' to the square at three o'clock, and I'm goin' wi' ye! How do we know it wasn't me she spoke to?" Both knew Miss Jean had not meant Peter Blair, but the bold Peter would not give up so easily, even if she had not so much as given him a second glance. Nearing the occupied bench, Peter spoke again.

"Are we just goin' to walk on by them, or are we goin' to say something?"

By this time Bruce was wishing he had stayed in his room. Maybe this Jean could be included among those his mother had taken such pains to warn him about. She had seemed a bit brazen!

"Do not speak to strange women, and never let the strong drink touch your lips!" had been Elspeth's warning, sounding exactly like her own father's words.

In the light of the small amount of knowledge he had at the time, Bruce's hearty laugh had rung through the room. "As if I would, even if I got the chance, eh, Gran'pa?" Andrew and Gran'pa exchanged glances. Neither laughed with him.

"Your mother is right, Bruce, lad, you won't have trouble to seek if you pay no attention to any of the two, wine and women!"

The grandfather nodded, sagely adding, "Never forget to pray. If ye couldna' take the Lord wi' ye someplace, then don't go yersel'."

"Could I take the Lord?" not realizing he thought out loud or that his companion could hear. Bruce could feel the ready flush fill his cheeks and neck as Peter turned in surprise at the words.

"Eh? What did ye say? I only asked if you were goin' to speak or if ye would walk right by!"

"You may do as you please. I'm going back to my room!" Walking quickly away from the scene, before Peter could stop him, Bruce ran back across the square. Peter, undecided about following him, hesitated only briefly, and with a shrug, he approached the girls. There would be plenty of chances to talk to this "thrawn hielandman" later on. Just now he was more interested in talking to "Bonnie Jean."

"Bonnie Jean" fumed, furiously angry with herself for allowing her emotions to run away from her in the dining room after dinner. On the other hand the opportunity of speaking to Bruce MacAlister alone, once university started, seemed remote indeed, so she had risked it. Now as she watched the subject of her attention disappear round the corner, the pent-up feelings of guilt and embarrassment erupted. She forgot her genteel upbringing and Granny's strict rules of conduct so much that when Peter Blair, outwardly sure but inwardly quaking, swept off his hat in a courtly bow, both he and Betsy received the next shock.

"Go and jump in the Clyde!" Snatching the inoffensive hat out of Peter's hand, Miss Bonnie Jean Irvine hurled it with all her might. The hat, caught in the wind, lazily wafted its way upward, to land jauntily askew on the head of no less imposing a stone horseman than Sir Walter Scott himself, for all Glasgow to see. Not waiting to find out what would happen next, she stamped angrily away, the loyal Betsy trailing behind. Betsy, still too surprised to speak, glanced back only once. What she saw would keep her and Cook laughing for many nights as they shared their late night cuppa, the strong, dark tea they both enjoyed. An admiring crowd gathered round the statue with the hat, and as usual with the good-natured Glaswegians, wending home from work in festive mood on such a braw Saturday afternoon, it was as good as a pantomime.

"Oh, Miss Jean, I'm fair winded. Could ye no' stop a minute and see what ye've done?" Betsy talked to thin air, however, and knowing that if Jean arrived back at the house without her, trouble would be brewing, she hastened her step again. As Betsy ran she thought, *Oh, well! If things go on like this, we'll have a grand term!*

9

Professor Angus Archibald Alexander was tired—tired of the interminable round of blank faces staring up at him from across the crowded room. There had been a time, so long ago that he scarcely recognized himself within the painful memory, when he regarded the sea of faces as more than blobs. His poetic soul had considered each one as an individual, a clean canvas waiting only the sweep of the oiled brush of his great words of wisdom to bring it to life. He knew not when this dream began to fade; he only knew it had vanished. Today, the most dreaded of all his days, would bring a fresh batch of faces, of these blank canvases, some eager, some bored, some there merely to please a parent or other patron. Few, if any, held that inner zeal, that burning inside to learn and then to speak of a living faith. Deep in his own heart, the teacher knew he was being unfair; and if this year such a one leaped out from the crowd and he did discern it, he feared his own warped zeal would hinder and quench rather than encourage and edify the student.

Stepping smartly through the legendary ivy-covered halls, the professor's smile remained grim. The tall, slightly stooped figure still retained a dignity of its own, although his gown showed many patched places and both sleeves had ragged edges. His snow-white hair contrasted strongly with his dark eyes, presenting a stunning and altogether attractive appearance of which he was either unaware or unheeding. The students he would face today would represent the final assemblage of hopefuls to come under his influence. He would see them through their four years, and then, thank God, he would be finished. He would have run the race. Obviously all who entered a race could not win. There must be runners-up to include those, like him, the Reverend A. A. Alexander, B.A., D.D., as mere also-rans. Resting his hand momentarily on the handle before opening the door to his classroom, his heart suddenly surged with renewed hope. Could this perhaps be the year? The thought became a prayer, "Maybe this last time, Lord!"

A hush descended on the room as the professor entered, and the young men waiting stood up as they had been instructed to do. The conversation, prior to this moment, had been fraught with guessing and trepidation. "Angry Angus," as his reputation described him, was still a legend. For Bruce MacAlister, this day marked an ending as well as a beginning—an ending of preparation and planning stretching as far back as memory would take him. For some of the others it meant a mere continuation of a time of sufferance, part of the growing-up process insisted upon by indulgent parents or sponsors. For such as those it made little difference what course they embarked upon.

A "hrumph," the never-to-be-ignored sound that would quickly become a signal to strike fear in the heart of even the most innocent in this group, broke the silence. Then, "As an indulgence—the only one I intend to make, I might add—seeing it's your first day away from your mammys, I will be writing on the blackboard. We will not trust to memory. You will find I make no allowances in this regard, so you will spend the next twenty minutes copying out what I or anyone whom I may delegate writes on the board. . . . The following will form your ten commandments while you are under my teaching. Now begin. We will assume the first two words of each exhortation to be: *Thou shalt!*"

Never be late.

Never be sick.

Never make excuses.

Never preach a private gospel.

Never argue with your teacher.

Never bring any sacred cows or personal shibboleths to class.

Never rant or rave.

Never imagine, in spite of what your mammy might have told you, that you are God's answer for Scotland's salvation or any other salvation.

Never take anything for granted.

Never offer an unasked-for opinion

Intent on writing, Bruce was not aware that he was under scrutiny for some considerable time. His brow wore the deep, furrowed frown so often smoothed away by his mother's hand as she recalled the same look on the two men who had influenced her life most. Bruce's inheritance was a double portion of the trait. Instinctively moving his hand now to cover up the notebook, he waited for the robed figure to speak.

"MacAlister, is it?"

Jumping to his feet, but not before turning over the notes, Bruce held out his hand.

"Bruce MacAlister, Dr. Alexander, sir!" The hand was ignored, and a fleeting memory of another such occasion flashed through Bruce's mind.

"Let me see what you've written!"

"But sir!"

"You've not observed the fifth commandment I see. You've a lot to learn, hielandman. I'll take the notebook. Now, if you please?" As he reached for the book Bruce snatched it up and held it close.

"No, I'm sorry, sir, but it's private!"

"Private is it? Private? No doubt you're writin' your letters to your Mammy, or is it your Flora MacDonald, in the time you're supposed to be taking notes on the rules of Glasgow University's faculty of theology. Nothing is private here!" The professor's voice had risen in his wrath, and the others in the room sat silent. The young man chosen to finish printing the "commandments" on the blackboard halted, his hand frozen in midair. The class held its breath.

"I'd finished the commandments so far, sir, and—"

"I'll have the notebook. If you've nothing to hide, then you've nothing to worry about!"

"No!"

"No, is it? No, is it? If you've no respect for me or the cloth I wear or the university I represent, then perhaps you'll agree if I tell you that to say no once might be permitted, making allowance for ignorance, but to say it twice is positive rebellion, and to say it thrice would be anarchy! Is it another Bonnie Prince Charlie we have here, or even a shade of Robert the Bruce himself?" A titter of nervous laughter followed this remark, to be instantly silenced as the irate man whirled, his gown ballooning out behind him, withering it with a glance.

"Silence! This is no time for levity! We have here a situation full of not just insolence but thrawn rebellion bordering on revolution. Only because it's your first day here will it be tolerated at all. However I'll make this a token lesson to seal the fact that the writings of the last hour are not just idle notes to while away the time. Hunter! Continue the writing on the board. I believe the next commandment might convince our noble hielandman and the rest of you with similar aspirations on individuality of this." Even as he taunted the young man, Angus Alexander cursed inwardly. He had placed himself in a position of no retreat, and he could not understand his own actions. Why did he have to behave so harshly? Even as he thought this, fearing he knew the answer, his voice continued without faltering, "You are not in the wee 'thackit' cottage school in the hielan' glen any more, you know. By what I'm led to understand, while there you were the shining light to all the township. Here you will need to prove yourself first. I will explain our deep interest in your notes. What you do during this class is our business, and we want to learn a bit from so distinguished a fellow. Now I'll have that notebook!" The last sentence came through teeth clenched together so tightly it sounded more like a hiss in this rage that went far beyond any reason. The two men stood facing each other. The older disillusioned and bitter against life, the younger as yet untried. The other occupants of the room were hushed and expectant, some with that thrill of excitement coursing deliciously through vein and sinew as they imagined how this would feel were they the objects of such wrath, others embarrassed and wishing it would end.

How long the impasse might have lasted would never be known had not a flurry of movement in the doorway caught their attention. Standing there in his full regalia of flowing robes, resplendent with the rich velvet stripes of his office, stood the rector himself, the Right Reverend Dr. David Ferguson. A gasp rose from the students. Some of them recognized the beetling brows from the portrait in the hall, while others, who knew not the face, perceived the significance of the visit from the style of robe and the awed attention. Angus whirled round to meet this new challenge. With face already crimson, he now felt a trickle of sweat on his forehead, and the hair on the back of his neck begin to rise. What could this visitation mean? "The Neb" never stopped in the homerooms without prior notice or invitation, especially not on opening day. Obviously unaware of the tension he had walked into, the great man began to speak, his question one of the trite remarks he was famous for, "What seems to be the matter, Dr. Alexander?"

Flustered and furious, mostly with himself but also with the young upstart whose stubbornness had put him in this position, Angus lied. "Nothing's the matter, Dr. Ferguson, just getting acquainted!" He would not presume to ask his superior why they were being honored by this historic visit. In theory the rector could come and go as he pleased, and it was unheard of for anyone, even Angus, who had been here for thirty years and had outlasted many like the man confronting him now, to question him.

"You may be seated!" The class members sat, albeit some uneasily on the edges of their hard benches, as the rector continued. Bruce, heart pumping and hands clammy, but still clutching tightly to his precious journal, sat, too, his lips moving in silent prayer.

"I apologize for disrupting your class this morning, Dr. Alexander, but I have a special reason. One of the honored graduates of our school and the son of a very dear friend of mine, Reverend Fraser Clegg, now a missionary in China, has written me, and enclosed with his letter is a note for one Bruce MacAlister. As I was passing this room I took a fancy to see this young man for myself, as Fraser has told me much of him. I also thought I would deliver the note personally."

To give Dr. Ferguson his due, he knew not what he did, and Bruce, although happy to receive word of Fraser, at this moment found himself praying most fervently, like King David in the Psalms, "Oh, for the wings of a dove that I might fly away." The collective indrawing of breath sounded loudly in the room and was followed by a stricken silence.

Belatedly the rector noticed the awkwardness and decided to take his leave. But first, "If Bruce MacAlister will step forward, I will give him his note and leave you to return to your studies. As your professor will no doubt be telling you, considering the immensity of the important task you are undertaking, you will need all your time!"

Bruce, looking first at Dr. Alexander and seeing nothing but plain disgust on his face, stood up and walked forward. This time he did not offer his hand: "I am Bruce MacAlister."

Belated wisdom entered the older man. Although supreme head of all he surveyed, there were unwritten laws and codes beyond which even he should not step. Had it not been for his excitement at hearing from Fraser after two years of silence, the other news from China being bad, he would never have broken the rule of protocol. Quickly he handed the note to Bruce and with no further words left the room.

The whole incident took about ten minutes, but it was to become historic, growing in size and dimension, depending on the teller. Bruce, not flying away or even being swallowed up by the wooden floorboards, returned to his place. Rage again engulfed Angus Alexander, and it was all he could do to keep from smashing the innocent face in front of him. Once before in his career a similar fury had caused him to lose control, and on that occasion a student, the son of a lord with every advantage known to man, had stood in this very room, wearing the same look of beatific naïveté Bruce MacAlister wore. That it was a look of purity, signifying a true calling, Angus knew very well. He knew because it was the calling that he had evaded and then fought so bitterly all his life. He was acting now in the only way open to his nature, and his watchers must never know of his inner torment. No one but he would know of the hours to be spent in agonized soul searching and self-flagellation that would come later when he reached the doubtful solace of his empty room.

"So I'm to remind ye of the immense importance of the course you are embarking upon. The dire responsibility of the task you are undertaking? Yes, I'll do that right enough. But first, to the ten commandments we will add this appendage: Thou shalt not expect to hold any special privilege because of who you know, be it the rector or Queen Victoria!" A nervous snigger ran through the room, to cease abruptly as the teacher spoke again: "The next list you will take note of is the one of the books to be read by the end of a fortnight. You will take them in turns and the first readers will be expected to. . . ." The remainder of the exhortation flowed round the room as Bruce, being careful not to appear inattentive and doubly careful not to be seen with any notes, tried his best to listen. When would it be over? Seemingly not yet. Once again he heard his name called.

". . . So seeing we have in our midst such rich talents of

rhetoric and the *cacoethes scribendi* so necessary in one desiring the cloth we all revere, one with such influence in high places, he, that is no other than our own hielan' laddy, Master Bruce MacAlister, will be the first to serve his fellows in this noble capacity!" Suddenly the man's bantering tone changed, and he hissed at Bruce. "MacAlister! You will read all four of Wesley's journals; you will write a detailed essay on your findings; and you will report back to the class in two weeks. Meanwhile do not neglect your other studies as outlined in the curriculum. We will soon discover if you are indeed endowed with more substance than what the spoon has put in you!"

10

"**M**an! There's just no excuse for you to sit here mopin' day in and day oot! So you're faraway from your highlands? Why Loch Lomond is on our very doorstep. I'll have you know it's the greatest of all lochs, with the ben standin' above it like a sentinel and all the braw islands. We could climb up and look out to the northwest, and you could let your imagination leap, when your eyes can see no further, to far Ben Nevis and your precious western isles." Peter's poetic license seemed to fall on deaf ears. For the past two weeks, ever since their arrival at Strathcona House and the episode in George Square, he had been trying to interest Bruce in some kind of activity apart from classes and homework. His other efforts to date having failed, he now appealed to the young highlander's obvious homesickness.

Bruce, with volume three of Wesley's journals spread open on the small marble table beside his bed, was not as intent on the heavy textbook as he should have been. In fact, he had heard every word spoken by Peter, his interest sparked by the mention of the famous loch. Still pretending to be deeply engrossed, he reached across the table, meaning to pick up his notebook. The flimsy structure, inadequate for the task, collapsed under his weight. His stiffness collapsed at the same time, and between great spurts of laughter, Bruce gasped, "All right! All right! I'll come with you. What will I need to bring?"

Peter, on the point of giving up, erupted into frenzied activity. It was Saturday morning, and the young men had adjourned to Bruce's room the moment breakfast was over. The meal, like all the meals since their first one, had been silent. Only the four students sat at table now, served by a tight-lipped Betsy. The promise of family feeling given on that faraway day of beginnings had come to naught. Bruce usually bent his head to say a quick grace over the food, while the morose Mr. Davidson would intone a melancholy one-line thank-you before they all hurried off to their various tasks.

This morning had seemed no different to Bruce, until, suddenly looking up, he caught a glimpse of a straying shaft of brilliant sunlight squeezing its way between the curtains shading the windows of the dining room. All at once the place changed miraculously, and a glow shimmered the silverware, causing it to dazzle his eyes for a moment as he reached out to fill his plate. It was then he began to feel the longing for Aribaig. On a day like this, as soon as his work was done, he would have taken Spicer, and together they would have roamed the hills. What scenery, what solitude, and what somehow-frightening grandeur of faraway crested peaks would have greeted his eyes. Leaving the farm and the town far behind, Bruce had oftimes felt the rush of tears and a painful gripping in his throat as he sat on a rock, the dog at his feet, gazing spellbound. Later, they would have wended their way homeward; filled with the delights of the day, they would have stopped to eat their piece at the mouth of a cave. Here his imagination would have soared, and he would have thought of the cave as maybe the very one to have hidden a prince in another century.

Bending now to pick up the scattered contents of the table, Bruce felt strangely at peace again. His new friend, Peter, was already shouting out orders gleefully. "I'll tell the maid we'll no' be back til' Sunday at suppertime. Roll up your other boots in the blanket, and tie it thegither wi' this twine. Everything else we need is in my pack sack. Oh, man, we'll be at the Lomond by teatime, easily!"

*　　*　　*

For a pair of hikers, they had not done much hiking yet, Bruce thought as the old coach made its rickety way along the barely discernible road. He smiled at the recollection of how his companion had haggled with the coachman. Eventually they reached an agreement that the two youths could travel on top of the coach with him, for the price of one, if they would load and unload the other passengers' bags and bundles from the "dickey." Now they were fast approaching a fork in the road, where they would leave the coach to continue its journey toward the seaports, while they turned their faces north to Loch Lomond and the town of Balmaha.

In a remarkably short time, the coach disappeared from their view, and the true hiking expedition began. According to Peter's rough and ragged map, they still had about ten miles of their journey on foot before they would reach their destination. Taking out his watch, Bruce noted it was only one o'clock, so their hopes remained high of being in Balmaha in time for tea. Peter's enthusiasm gradually infected Bruce, and he found himself stirring with the excitement of the adventure. Resolving to simply let go and enjoy it, he soon joined his new friend in the song that seemed most appropriate for the occasion: "Oh ye'll tak' the high road an' I'll tak' the low road, An' I'll be in Scotland before ye; But I an' my true love will never meet again, on the bonnie, bonnie banks of Loch Lomond."

The bonnie banks were ablaze with a most glorious sunset when the two hungry, happy hikers limped into the hostelry at Balmaha, too late for tea, but the friendly landlord soon had a kettle boiled and a table spread for them.

"Fittin' fare for Prince Charlie himsel'," Peter looked over at Bruce as they sat down to the meal.

Bruce responded gently by saying, "Heavenly Father, forgive us for forgetting, even for so short a time, that You have all things in Your hands. Now we thank You for this good day and this food, which is Your bounty. Bless all who reside here this night and keep us safe. In Jesus' name, amen." The silence in the room as he finished speaking brought his eyes open in time to watch the varied reactions. Peter, slightly red in the face, began quickly to fill his plate. Several patrons smiled into their tankards, while the landlord himself grinned broadly.

The scene in the MacIntyre dining room was quite another story this Saturday teatime. It being Betsy's day off, that meant Jean would serve tea, and this was her first appearance in the public section of the boarding house for two weeks now. She had only one boarder to serve, along with her grandmother, who also had come out of seclusion.

The old lady was speaking, "A most delicious tea, although I say it myself. Give Cook my compliments, won't you, Jean?"

"Yes, Granny. Will you excuse me now, please? I'll be back after you are finished, to help Cook wash up."

"You ate so little, Jean. Won't you have some of that tasty ham or a sausage roll?"

"No, thank you, Granny, I'm still not hungry."

Mrs. MacIntyre made as if to protest some more but thought better of it and subsided into her chair. Turning to the lone man seated almost morosely on her left side, she inquired, "And how are you settling in, Mr. Leekie?" In spite of herself, Jean could not help smiling as she quietly slipped through the door. Poor Willie Leekie. In this mood Granny could easily keep him talking, or more likely listening, for an hour or so. The smile showed only a sad, faint shadow of the girl's normally happy countenance. Jean Irvine had been born in 1855, the only child of Cameron and Jessica Irvine (née MacIntyre). At the time of her birth, the Irvines had been in service in India, and it had been there that Jean had spent her childhood, growing up in the midst of the extremes of that land, with its lavish richness and its heart-wrenching poverty that was the Punjab in those days. Having the blessed fortune of being home on furlough during the Delhi mutiny of '58, they had been spared that dreadful ordeal from which few British escaped alive. So Jean had been three years old when she met Granny for the first time. It had been a meeting of kindred spirits. Being of like temperaments did not cause these two that conflict which, according to the new thought being expounded on the subject of temperaments, it ought to have. On the contrary each knew she had met her match, and both behaved accordingly. Occasionally Granny, being the senior, was forced to exert that seniority by way of the rod of discipline, but this was tacitly understood and made no difference to the relationship or the mutual admiration.

When Jean returned to India, at the age of eight, the two were firmly established in a love that went much deeper than mere family blood required and that would last a lifetime. The association continued through long, monthly newsletters, a joy for each to both write and receive. Returning to her room now, Jean resumed the task she had been working on during the two weeks of self-imposed exile: going through her letters. Now that she was a grown woman, there were some things she would not need to keep, but her idea to clear out the rubbish was not happening. She would sort a pile of papers, one stack for the fire and one for the souvenir box. Then there was the other box, a secret even from Granny: the big envelope full of notes from her diary and the notes for her book. She would place a scrap of paper on the pile for keeping, then quickly grab it and scrunch it up for the waste pile. Then she would sigh and smooth it out to replace it in the envelope marked STRICTLY PRIVATE, JEAN IRVINE. One such paper was in her hand; it had already been crushed and smoothed at least three times. She just could not decide. "Dear Granny," she read now. "Can you please take me home? The girls are all nice here at Winchley House, and so are *some* of my teachers, but they are teaching me things that I learned in India from Raju Singh when I was six years old. I try to listen, as you said, but it is torture. Could I not learn at home from you until I am old enough for college? Please Granny, oh, please!" She smiled again, remembering. Granny had not needed that second *please*. At that time the MacIntyre Establishment for Respectable Young Men, Students of Theology and Medicine, had temporarily relaxed its rule of men only. One afternoon another young lady had arrived on the doorstep of Strathcona House.

Faye Felicity Gordon had not been unexpected, as a few weeks previously Beulah had received a letter from her good friend Isabel Gordon. Faye Felicity's mother had been married quite late, and surprise of surprises for one so richly endowed with all the riches this world could offer as well as extremely high intellectual gifts, had married a farmer, who carried her off into the wilds of the Yorkshire dales. The couple, so unlikely and yet so well suited to each other, proceeded to fill their large farmhouse with healthy young Gordons. That Isabel was busy and happy Beulah had no doubt, and if she sometimes read between the lines a wistful longing for intellectual stimulation, the discerning and wise friend replied with a fat package of books and papers giving out all the doings of their mutual contemporaries. Faye Felicity became the final edition of the Gordon progeny and the only female. She and her six brothers had been taught by their mother to read and write before going to the village school, for whatever education it offered. The boys had been content, as each in his turn reached an age where he could leave school and begin his real-life work, to join the ranks of the country's food providers. Almost resembling an assembly line, each one, on reaching maturity, had married a girl from the village or the surrounding area. A ritual had begun when the eldest received a farm of his own for a marriage gift.

Donald Gordon was a prosperous man, not lettered but knowing his business of farming thoroughly and having himself inherited much. Finally only Faye had been left at home. Very quickly she had learned all the village school had to teach her, then all her mother had to offer. The parents had been at a loss. A bewildered father had brought in a grand piano. She had mastered that by the time she was eleven years old. Every book that came into the farmhouse had been literally devoured by Faye Felicity. She could recite whole books of the Bible and not merely chapters and verses. Thrilling her father, even if he did not understand how she came to that decision all by herself, this girl prodigy had announced quite matter-of-factly one day that not only did she know most of the New Testament by heart, she believed it by heart, implicitly. There could be no doubt of it.

Isabel's cry had ever been, "What shall we do with her?" Talking to Beulah on one of her quick excursions to Glasgow, she had bewailed the fact that her only girl, although it would be cruel to suggest she was ugly, was certainly not pretty. Very small in stature, yet she had large, heavy bones that gave her a top-heavy look undiminished by the thick knot of dark brown hair that always seemed to pull the girl's head back in an ungainly fashion. The best of medical care had failed to produce any help for the cruelly myopic eyes, other than a pair of thick, round, pebbly eyeglasses, rimmed with gold but nonetheless owly. One redeeming feature of the face was a gently curving, sweet-lipped mouth, over perfect, if overlarge, teeth. Her smile could only be described as angelic. In response to both the spoken and the unspoken pleas of her friend, Beulah MacIntyre had invited, no urged, that Faye Felicity be allowed to stay at her house while they stormed the gates of learning to find a place for this enigma. That she would surpass student and teacher alike was not mentioned at this point. Jean's letter had arrived by the afternoon post, just as Beulah was about to pour tea. She and Faye Felicity had been in the small private sitting room known by the student boarders as "the dragon's lair."

"Why did I not think of it before? Of course! Faye Felicity, my dear, how would you like to be a private tutor and continue where the paragon Raju Singh left off with her education?" The intonation in her voice as she had spoken the name betrayed to her listener a degree of her deep-seated feelings—if not downright envy, then at least a tinge of prejudice. A smile of understanding, far beyond her years, had passed over the younger woman's face.

"Oh yes, Auntie, I would like that!" Very faintly, the

Yorkshire accent had filtered through the pure English learned at her mother's knee, but it had been there just the same.

Beulah had continued to outline her plans: "I will telegraph that school at once, and we will travel together, you and I, to bring Jean home. We can leave early in the morning and be back by teatime. Paddy McShane can take us in his brougham. After all, Stirling is not that far away!"

So it happened. The three had returned, tired, dusty, but happy. Jean had been hysterical with excitement, only slightly subdued by the small fear that Granny's respect for Faye Felicity always brought out in her. Her emotions matched the great feeling of achievement that had flowed through Beulah at the so obvious and timely solution to the two problems.

Jean quickly proved her excellence as a pupil, although of course she had not been nearly in the same category as Faye Felicity, who had soon become adjusted to her role as teacher. The household had settled into a new routine, heralding an interesting time of great intellectual stimulation. The three young students resident for the year 1867 had been blessed in ways that they, in their ignorance, took for granted but would have amazed those gone ahead of them or even those who followed after, could they have known.

Beulah had positively bloomed in this atmosphere. As for Faye Felicity Gordon, she had found her forte in helping to fill the mind of her young charge with some of her own knowledge. Until then her outlets for the things she herself absorbed, seemingly without limit, had been few. Suddenly she found that sharing made her desire for more learning a tangible thing as she began to hear firsthand about places and peoples before known to her only from books. One afternoon soon after the beginning of this ideal situation, Jean had brought up the subject of India. Immediately Faye had asked: "He must have been a really special person, your Raju?"

Enthusiastically Jean had agreed, completely missing the slightly quizzical look on her new friend's face. "Oh, yes, very special, although sometimes I feel that Granny doesn't want me to talk about him. I remember a letter she wrote once. It was when she was telling me about you, when you stayed for a holiday last year. Oh, I'm sorry, Faye, I should not say these things."

"What things? I'm sure anything your granny said about me would be all right for me to hear."

"Yes, I was thinking how I'm not supposed to keep talking about Raju so much, and then when I wrote to Granny telling her about him, I asked her if she always said your two names together, the way she wrote them. Oh, dear! Now I am talking too much about—"

"But I want to hear about Raju Singh. I am sure your granny won't be angry if I tell her I asked you especially."

"Well, he didn't know where his father and mother were. Our cook says he picked the small boy up out of the rubbish bin one day and. . . . Oh, I better not tell you that part, just what I knew about him from our bungalow. Anyway he, that is Raju, came to us from the missionary compound. He was to teach me English and composition and all that. Isn't it funny how you are taking up where he left off? He is a Christian, and he taught me things from the Bible as well. Like Granny was the first to teach me about Jesus loving me and how I should love Him in return. Raju gave me lessons about 'all things work together for good to them that love God,' so I try always to love Him. Oh dear, I think I've mixed this all up, but do you know what I mean, Faye?"

"I think I know what you mean!" Faye, trying hard not to laugh out loud, decided maybe this was enough for the time being.

"You know, Jean, that book we just finished, how would you like to start another one by the same author?"

"I would, but do we have any more?"

"I'm not sure, but anyway I think we should ask Auntie if we can start going to the library for more books. We have almost exhausted her supply."

So had begun an almost daily excursion. Together they

would leave the house on George Street, sometimes chaperoned by the aged Lanarkshire-Irishman Paddy McShane, but more often, as the weather started to improve, just the two of them. They would set off walking briskly westward, sometimes taking in the beauties of nature, but mostly hurrying on their way to the university at Kelvinside. While there, they would spend hours happily engrossed and forgetting time, until a thoroughly disgruntled custodian of the precious treasury of books and artifacts would announce, "Closin' time, ladies!" and they would quickly choose the two volumes they were allowed to borrow on the strength of the auspicious name of Mrs. Beulah MacIntyre, widow of the Reverend Dr. Archibald MacIntyre, so long a member of the faculty of this very university. Then the girls would hurry out to board a tram car for the return to the house, quite often shaving their time close to missing tea!

This idyllic situation lasted for close to a year, and all three females involved made the most of it. If a lonely mother on the Yorkshire dales wondered why she suddenly missed her daughter and questioned the matter, she never said a word aloud. Within her heart the eternal *Why, God?* may have echoed.

One day Faye Felicity had announced she would now begin her nursing training. As no one had ever suspected her of such ambitions, the surprise was great. It seemed that while Jean had pursued the intricacies of mathematics and physics, Faye had been doing some research of her own, reading about such persons as Dr. David Livingstone and Florence Nightingale. The first letter to Yorkshire had brought an irate Isabel storming to Glasgow, her list of reasons clutched tightly in her leather gauntlets. It was all to no avail. Miss Faye Felicity Gordon had made up her mind.

"I'm going to the mission field, Mummy, and that's that. I would have gone without training, but as I read about these places I saw where they need more than spoken words!" After that letters had passed between Glasgow and Yorkshire and London. For a time it had seemed the subject would be closed, but then one day a large brown envelope importantly stamped and addressed to Miss Faye Felicity Gordon had arrived in George Street. Fond if tearful farewells had echoed through Glasgow's Central Station, and amid clouds of steam and cindery smoke, the London Caledonian had departed, with the determined young Yorkshire lass firmly ensconced in a private bedroom apartment. Queen Victoria herself could not have been better served.

She would begin nurse's training in London at the famous Florence Nightingale School in St. Thomas's Hospital. Then she'd go on to the London Mission Society to prepare for Calcutta.

The next day a family conference had taken place in George Street, culminating in a most satisfactory solution, at least as far as Jean was concerned. For two hours each weekday morning Jean would study by herself. Each afternoon Granny would review the morning's work and assign the next day's lesson. The rest of the day Jean would help in the house, learning housewifely tasks before going off with the maid or the cook, whoever could spare the time and felt inclined. Once a week, usually Mondays, they would proceed to the manse and the Right Reverend Charles Broughton, a friend of her deceased grandfather, would teach the girl for an hour on things spiritual. This old man's depth of scriptural knowledge, which he used in a daily application in his real life, would prove a real inspiration to the girl. Other helpers in the all-round education of Jean Irvine came and went. One year Granny boarded a professsor of English, and he had seemed pleased to give Jean examinations equal to university entrance requirements in his subject. His remarks that she would pass but by no means excel in English had caused the two women much amusement. At eighteen, still hoping for acceptance in the university's teacher training program, but in no particular hurry, Jean had been content to just let the days pass. Mummy and Daddy would be home in a few years, this time for good, and life seemed pleasant enough, if lacking in excitement. Until now that was—until that moment of impulsive madness, when she had made a suggestion, completely foreign to her nature, and had actually frightened away the very person she wanted to become acquainted with.

What, oh, what would he think of her?

On this day when Bruce MacAlister was discovering middle Scotland and learning that other parts of Scotland besides his beloved western highlands had beauty and grandeur almost equal to them, Jean Irvine and her granny had a little "talk."

Glancing now at the small clock on her bureau, she almost cried out. Raju, who had bought the thing for a couple of baksheesh one day in the native marketplace, would know what to do next. Suddenly hearing her granny's voice just outside her room, on the landing, Jean quickly gathered up the various letters and notes, thrusting them untidily into a shoe box and pushing it under the bed. When Beulah sailed into the room, a few seconds later, she appeared to be busy knitting.

Taking in everything at a glance, Beulah said, "Jean, would you put your knitting away and pay attention to what I have to say, please?"

"Sorry, Granny, I was wool gathering!" The unintended pun brought a faint smile to her lips, but her grandmother was not to be sidetracked.

"During the last two weeks you have moped about the house with a faraway look in your eyes. At first I thought it would quickly pass or that it was your annual bout of homesickness for India and Raju, but this is not what I think now! No! It occurs to me that this dreamy sadness has been evidenced in your behavior only since the new boarders have taken up residence with us. Now your face is betraying you, so all I need to find out is which one is it? Which of these young rapscallions is affecting you this way?" A small sound escaped Jean, but whether in protest or agreement Beulah could not tell. The crimson flag in each cheek spoke volumes. Marveling at her granny's ability to read the signs, Jean still showed no emotion and spoke no word.

Placing the knitting down on the counterpane of her crisply white bed, she waited, eyes downcast and head bent in an attitude of submission that also was foreign to her nature. Granny was neither deceived nor put off.

"Jean, did you hear me, or am I merely talking to the furniture?"

"I heard you, Granny." Silence reigned again. Suddenly Beulah moved in.

"Jeannie, my wee pet, what is it? You can tell me. Tell Granny!" The dam burst. Jean, waiting for recrimination or scolding, maybe even for a punishment of some kind, because Betsy, good friend as she might be, would not have been quiet about the hat business in the square, was totally unprepared for the tender notes of compassion in her grandmother's voice. That wall, so carefully built up to hide tender feelings, crumbled.

"Oh, Granny, I don't even know what it is or why I feel so funny. It's like a pain in my throat, and it takes my breath away and my appetite and, oh, Granny . . . !" the last was a wail of woe, and the floodgates opened.

11

"Peter, it's glorious! Oh, man it is, it's glorious!" The soft, peaty tones of the highlands escaped easily today as Bruce spoke.

Peter preened like a peacock, with an air of ownership giving the impression that he, Peter Thomson Blair, could take full credit for all this beauty. With studied nonchalance he replied, "Wait 'til you see it further north as it narrows and the east shore is in full view, but for the now I'm beat!" So saying he threw himself down on the spongy bank, having first taken time to clear it of small rocks and sticks. Bruce stood gazing across the water. Then he lowered himself gently to the ground beside Peter, keeping his eyes on the glorious vista of mile upon mile of silver water leading upward to whispers of woodland as they blended into the faraway majestic mountains, with their white heads and purple shoulders beginning to vanish in the evening haze. Seated there in the heather, chin resting on his cupped hands, Bruce seemed prepared to remain until he could no longer see, but Peter had other ideas.

"We should go back now and turn in early before this Scotch mist soaks us to the skin; then we'll rise before daylight and watch the sunrise. It's better to watch the sunrise from here and the sunset from Balmaha." Even as Peter spoke Bruce felt a dampness rising from the mossy ground. Reluctantly he heaved himself up.

"I thought we were to be roughing it by sleeping in your pup tent and not in yon luxurious inn?"

"Oh, well! It's your first time, and Willie Taggert would be astonished if he heard you call his humble establishment a luxurious inn. Anyway he's only charging us a shilling a night for bed and breakfast, with a high tea thrown in for 'bountiful measure,' as he so poetically says it. Makes it worthwhile not to have to bother with the tent or the cookin'." Mention of food and the sudden onset of darkness caused them to quicken their steps. Bruce felt tired, and he was eagerly looking forward to a good meal and all that the morrow might bring. Sinking into the surprisingly soft mattress—could it be down feathers?—before sleep overtook him he found his thoughts not to be of the bonnie green banks and braes of Loch Lomond, but of a certain bonnie red-haired lass in Glasgow, named Jean. Would she be out to serve the tea tomorrow night, when they returned? At last he admitted to himself alone how much he hoped she would be.

Crying her heart out on the black satin bosom, so often a place of solace in Jean Irvine's childhood, she had visualized Granny and herself both rushing about, maybe sending for Paddy McShane's "jauntin' car" as he called his brougham, before speeding off to the place where Bruce and Peter tramped the moors. After all, Granny could take care of everything! The utter foolishness of this idea broke over her now as she sat waiting while Granny prayed.

Beulah was not above including a favorite text and even a little sermon in her prayers. This evening she used the verse describing Jesus calming the troubled waters merely by stepping in the disciples' boat. Then she asked Jean to say the Twenty-third psalm. Jean recited obediently, wishing she could be whisked away beside certain still waters—the waters of Loch Lomond, where, so Betsy had told her, the two students were spending the weekend. Quietness in the room told Jean that Granny had finished praying and was looking at her intently.

"Jean, move back to your chair now, please. I have something else to tell you! And I want you to listen carefully." Smoothing out the front of her dress, she continued, almost in a low voice, "Oh, yes! You will be educated my dear, and I myself will prepare you for much more than your mother knows about, much more than she, I am sorry to say, was prepared for herself." Wondering, Jean waited.

"Your mother—or I should say, of course, your *parents*—sent you home to me five years ago with the object of your receiving an education. Although it was never stated in so many words, you and I both know they had some kind of establishment in mind. When our first attempt at boarding school failed, we were more than fortunate—I call it God's providence—in having that year with Faye Felicity!" Beulah stopped for breath, and Jean's mind clutched irrelevantly at the thought of Granny always giving Faye Felicity both her names.

Granny spoke on. "Although your mother doubted it at the time," by now all pretense about Jean's father being interested in his only child's education was forsaken, "later, when we sent the results of your tests given by Mr. Bacon, she appeared satisfied for a while. Yesterday's letter indicates she is having further thoughts on the matter. In short we are to begin again our search for a seat of learning that will accept a young female like yourself. Your mother was able to attend Queen's College in London, under another provision of God and only because your grandfather was teaching at University College for those two years." Beulah refrained from mentioning how Jessica had firmly stated that if all else failed Jean must rejoin her parents in India. "Now, for this present dilemma, we must make a list of the choices available before we speak of what is acceptable to all of us!" Jean's sigh echoed softly. Granny's legendary lists could take hours and always preceded changes, usually difficult ones. Jean scrunched further down in her chair, prepared for the long session. Granny, so particular with grammar, was inclined to speak long words with remote meanings, and all of Saturday evening stretched dolefully before her.

"First of all, Jean, I want to educate you on some facts about life itself. I am ashamed to admit it, but because of some foolish form of so-called delicacy—more likely prudery—I have refrained from telling you the facts about life and its beginnings. You see dear, before a—"

"Granny!"

"Jean, I must ask you not to interrupt me. There will be time to ask questions when I'm finished."

"But Granny, before you say any more let me tell you there is no need. You see, I know all about that!" A stunned gasp escaped Beulah.

"But how can you know what I am going to say? You have hardly been out of my sight since the day I brought you home from the boarding school in Stirling, and you were only twelve years old then. What do you mean?"

"Remember I lived in India all those years. I learned a lot there!"

"Your mother told you about the cycle of life?" Shocked incredulity registered in the old lady's voice.

"Oh, no, not Mummy, it was Raju! I made him explain it to me after I watched him helping Larissa, and I—"

"Pray begin at the beginning, child. I am at a loss to know of whom and what you speak."

"Larissa was my friend, but only Raju and I knew about her. She's about two years older than I, but much smaller. Her mother was dead, and her father was a Sepoy attached to Daddy's regiment. During the day she would sit and listen to Raju as he taught me. When the lessons were over, she and I would play together until Ayah called me for lunch, or tiffin. Then one day she didn't come. The rainy season had started, and when I asked Raju about her, he told me she would be back when the rain stopped. I didn't think the weather would bother Larissa, but Raju always knew about these things better than I, so I didn't say any more. About a month after that—I remember it was one of those heavy, black days when you know a storm is coming—Raju was giving me my lesson in the summerhouse. You remember how I told you the difference between your summerhouse and the one we had on our compound? Well it was really only an extension of the rest of the house, but the walls only came halfway up, with a breezeway leading to the main house. There was no breeze that day. Granny, I remember this all so clearly I can hear it still. I heard someone whisper Raju's name. A small, dirty beggar boy was peeping round the side of the railing. Raju signaled the dirty child to leave, before Ayah or Mummy saw him, but he would not go. I knew, too, that he had no right to be there. Speaking in a whisper, I asked Raju what the strange boy wanted. I knew most of the regular beggars who came to the door for baksheesh, but I had never seen this one before. He began to talk quickly to Raju. I could only understand one word, 'Rissa. I looked round to see if Ayah heard, but she was still asleep, so I turned back to try to hear what this beggar knew about my friend.

"Sepoys and other troopers paraded all day and seemed to be everywhere, so he had to keep hidden. Remember the rebellion had been only a few years before that?"

"I remember!" Beulah's voice sounded weak as she tried not to imagine the scene being so vividly described by Jean. *Why the girl has experienced more in her seventeen years than I have in my seventy, and here am I trying to tell her the facts of life.* Jean was still talking.

"So when Raju got up to follow the beggar boy—Asha was his name—he signaled me to be quiet and to stay with Ayah. I signaled back no and followed them. He could do nothing about it without making a fuss, and I knew it. If that happened, we would all be in trouble. So he let me come. Both of us risked not only Mummy's wrath, but Daddy's terrible anger; I still shudder at the thought of what might have happened if they ever found out how we left the compound that day. All the native servants knew of secret ways to get in and out, and we left by one of these. The scabby urchin led us to a place I won't describe to you, Granny. You might get upset!" Beulah moaned softly as she reached for her lavender-soaked hanky. *Upset!* If she could keep from swooning, it would prove a miracle.

"We had to bend over to enter through the tiny opening covered with old sacking. Inside, lying on the floor, was my friend Larissa, and she was hurt! The rags she lay on were covered with blood, and oh, Granny, I received an education in the next few minutes. Even Raju got angry with me and began to issue instructions after he told me to stop my silly talking and crying. Nobody would help Larissa. Her father had thrown her out because the man who did the terrible thing to her was a white man and her father was an Indian sergeant. The women of her acquaintance threw rocks at her if she came near them, and finally she had gone to this cave in the hills. The boy, Asha, had become frightened and come for Raju when—"

"Oh, Jean, stop! Stop! I canna stand any more." Jean's eyes were dark with the memory of all she had seen that far-off day and of the suffering of her friend. Beulah, in a state of shock at all she was hearing, choked out the words to halt Jean, but the girl continued as if the interruption had never been.

"Next day I asked Raju, no, I demanded that he tell me all the things I did not understand about Larissa's illness. At first he refused to speak of it, but when I threatened to ask Mummy, he told me. Granny, I made him tell me how that little dead thing that looked like a wax doll, even smaller than my own dolls, got into Larissa's body. Why it made her ill. Why she could not tell me about it. After all, was I not her friend? So Raju explained it all to me. But first he made me promise a solemn promise that I would tell no one else, and I never have, until now. He drew diagrams on our school blackboard, so that I would be left in no doubt. After that he also told me how it need not be the awful experience that had been Larissa's. He said that in God's plan for men and women, in a true marriage, that this act could be beautiful. At the time this was hard for me to believe, but knowing Raju—he never lies, you know—I thought maybe it would be true. I resolved never to find out. I still had some questions for poor Raju, like, 'If your God is so great, why did my friend have to suffer all that? Why, if it is not God's plan, could her body not wait until the right time and person before starting to reproduce as you told me?' I pray I shall never forget what he told me then. He said until 'mankind,' with evil predominating in their hearts as they live godless lives, change from the inside and desire good instead of evil, the innocent will suffer. He also assured me that one day right will prevail over might and said that should be our daily prayer."

Beulah had closed her eyes during the last part of this long tale, but she was not asleep. Silently she thanked God for this Raju, asking forgiveness for all her wrong attitudes about him. Belatedly she saw how God's answer to her fervent prayers for her grandchild's protection in yon faraway heathen land had taken the form of Raju. Unashamed now, her tears flowed, and for the second time that day, she pulled Jean close.

After a time she said, "We won't bother with the lights tonight. Jump into your bed, and I'll bring you a hot drink. Everybody else with any sense in this house is asleep this long while. We will continue our discussion about your formal education in the morning. It must be settled soon."

Jean snuggled down in her pillows, drowsy after drinking the hot milk and knowing in her heart there would be no more talk of her leaving Strathcona House for the present. Before sleep claimed her, she resolved tomorrow she would start to help Betsy with the serving again, beginning at teatime. She had been in hiding long enough.

During the night the Scotch mist soon changed to a heavy downpour. Peter woke to that steady drumming on the pantiles of the roof of the inn, recognized by every lowland Scot wherever he is. His loud groans woke Bruce.

"We'll not see the sun this day, my braw hielan' laddie!" His cheerful tones belied the words.

"What? Oh, well, we had a good view of its glory last night, so I'm not complaining. Only what should we do now? Glad I am, too, that we're not in yon wee tent!"

"I told you you could trust me. As for what to do, our breakfast is paid for, and I do believe I smell bacon frying. Throw off dull sloth, my man, and let us hie to the culinary heights—or should it be depths?—without further ado."

Breakfast over and their account with the hospitable Willie settled, the two looked at each other. A quick foray to the front door had sent them both scurrying back to the huge open hearth, accompanied by cries of anguish from some of the other patrons as the gale-force wind caught the smoke and whirled it round the room. But the door's opening had also brought a familiar clamor to Bruce's ears.

"I hear the kirk bells. If I knew where they were coming from, I would make a run for it. I do want to go."

"That's the chapel bells you hear, my son, but if the desire of your heart is to worship the Lord in spirit and in truth, ye need go nae further than this very room. Within the hour there'll be a readin' from the Word in this place." An elderly man had detached himself from the group round the fire and was approaching Bruce and Peter, where they were now seated on the wide window ledge. Holding out his hand to Bruce, the gentleman continued, "George Bennett is my name, and although not of the cloth myself, I've the privilege of servin' the Lord in the capacity of deacon in the 'Fellowship Brethren.' " Bruce accepted the handshake silently, reluctant to commit himself further. A sudden commotion at the door spared him from replying. A great flurry of foot stamping, umbrella shaking, and cloak removings announced the arrival of a sizable party. Bruce correctly assumed this to be the Fellowship Brethren. Turning to Peter, he was in time to see that young man disappear in the direction of the stairs. He made a move to go with Peter but stopped for a moment as if listening to something. All at once he felt compelled to accept the invitation, overwhelmed with a knowledge that he was exactly where he was supposed to be. Having prayed for a worship service by merely expressing a want to go to one, a worship service had come to him. Putting aside all his misgivings, he followed Mr. Bennett.

Betsy Degg returned from her half-holiday to a completely changed Miss Jean. In fact the change seemed to be affecting everybody. Sunday's duties included only strictly necessary jobs, so she and Jean were able to go for a short stroll after dinner. Delighted at the difference, Betsy could not help remarking to Miss Jean. "Oh, I'm that glad ye're feelin' better, Miss Jean, and more like yersel', so I am, and not just for the help ye are to me, either!"

Jean laughed merrily. "I'm glad, too, Betsy. Although I haven't been away anywhere, I feel as if I've just returned from a long journey. Now I think of it, I must thank you for not speaking of the time I threw the hat!"

Wisely Betsy refrained from further remarks about that. Maybe some other time she would tell Miss Jean about the laugh she and Cook had shared about the episode, but not today. Inclining her head, she changed the subject, "I wonder how many we should set for the night, Miss Jean. Mr. Blair said he and Mr. MacAlister would be back for tea, but I've a feelin' he meant supper. They speak a bit different from Fifeshire, don't they?"

"Yes, they do, Betsy, and different again is the speech from the western highlands, but we'd better hurry up, as I feel raindrops and we have walked further than usual." She turned away to hide the telltale blush at the mention of Mr. MacAlister, but Betsy had seen enough. Another tidbit for their late teatime: Miss Jean was sweet on the tall highlander. Out of breath but only slightly damp, the two girls entered the house on George Street by the back way just as the grandfather clock in the hall chimed the hour of four o'clock.

Betsy asked her question again as the two met in the dining room to set the places. "How many for then, Miss Jean?" As if on signal the side door burst open, and the unmistakable sounds of the travelers' return came to their ears.

Peter was speaking, "I told ye, Bruce, man, we'd be in plenty of time. Dae ye not smell that ham?"

"Sshh, Peter, ye'll disturb the whole house if ye haven't already. Yes, I do smell the ham, and I'm ready for it, too! Hurry up, or we might still be too late."

As the voices faded Beulah motioned to Jean not to sound the gong yet. They waited.

Mrs. MacIntyre did not comment on their lateness for tea, but Bruce had noticed the changed atmosphere, confirmed when the old lady began to ask questions about their hiking expedition. When Bruce mentioned Mr. George Bennett, she exclaimed, "George Bennett? It must be the same one! My husband knew him well. In fact he was a candidate for the ministry before. . . . Oh, well, I must write him a note of thanks for his kindness to those of my household, even those temporarily so. Possibly he would accept an invitation to tea some afternoon soon. Jean, remind me to write tomorrow. Mr. MacAlister, would you be so kind as to return thanks for the food?"

The ice was broken, and the household relaxed with a sigh of relief. Only the most insensitive could have missed the significance of Beulah's remarks. They could all settle down as a family, for this term at least. Later, in his room, Bruce ruefully picked up his textbook from where he had thrown it. Could that have been only yesterday? His remarks to Peter about the extra load of homework came back to him now. Blatantly he had regaled his friend with the fact that he loved history and would welcome the challenge. Inwardly he blessed Fraser Clegg for the grounding in the Wesley journals received when Fraser tutored him. The Christian apologetics and comparative religions were another matter, but he decided to apply Gran'pa's advice of "one thing at a time." It was the Lord's advice, too, so it must be good: ". . . sufficient unto the day. . . ." He had a lot to make up, but what did it matter? She had smiled at him. Pausing every now and then to bask in his content, Bruce laughed silently. He had been right with the first impressions. He was going to like it here.

12

"**D**ugald is awful late today!" Elspeth's voice sounded peevish, and Gran'pa and Andrew, coming in hoping dinner would soon be ready, knew that the remark needed no answer. Pacing back and forth to the kitchen window for the past hour had not interfered with her meal preparations, and soon the steaming plates of broth were placed in front of them. If privately each man thought the postie not so late, he kept quiet about it. Wednesday usually brought a letter from Bruce, but if it arrived one or even two days late, it made little difference to the peaceful life and work of the croft.

"Here he comes now, wife, a wee late maybe, so he'll have a drop broth and a bannock raither than just a cup o' tea." But Elspeth was off through the door and across the yard before he finished speaking. Dugald waved the envelope while she waited, trying hard to hide her impatience. The postie would have his say first.

"Aye, oor lad is faithfu'. That'll be the third letter in as many weeks. A just hope he keeps it up. This yin's got a strange envelope though. It says "King's Head, Balmaha!" He turned the precious missive over as he spoke. It was all Elspeth could do to keep from snatching it, but there was more to come. Dugald knew where Balmaha was. "Aye, Balmaha, it's on the Lomondside. A mind fine once when I. . . ." Desperately Elspeth reached for the letter, but Dugald would not be done out of his triumph so easily. Before he could continue his story, however, Andrew, closely followed by Gran'pa Bruce, appeared at the kitchen door.

"It's yersel', Dugald. Come away in and have some broth. Am I hearin' right that thon crysants o' yours are the running favorite for a ribbon in the flower show?"

This was too much for Dugald. Turning to the speaker, he called out, "A ribbon is it? Man, they'll take first prize easily!" He handed Elspeth her letters as he spoke. With barely a glance at the rest, she quickly took up the letter from her son.

The men waited for "afters," but no cake was forthcoming. A preoccupied Elspeth still pondered over the letter, moving from press to table and back as if in a dream. Having exhausted the subject of the flower show and then the weather, Andrew and Gran'pa Bruce exchanged smiles.

Finally Andrew spoke: "Did I not know it was the son writin', I would suspect a lass had just received her first love letter!"

Postie took up the joke, "Oh, aye, indeed, and the farawaw look in the eye would gar ye think it came fae the other side o' the world, if no' another world a'thegither!"

This remark startled Elspeth out of her dreamy state. Giving herself a little shake, she smiled. "You three! I'll read it to you in a minute, but it's just so strange." She put the letter beside her place and proceded to dish up the steaming bowls of rice pudding, such a favorite with her menfolk. No more banter came forth as they each picked up a spoon, determined to do it the justice it deserved. Three pairs of eyes swiveled toward Elspeth.

Finally Gran'pa spoke softly, "Is it the lassie?"

"Oh, no! He doesn't mention the lassie much, not exactly." More puzzled than ever, the men watched her, spoons poised in midair. She would explain in her own way.

"It will be better if I read it all to you out loud, and then you can decide for yourselves what you think it means. 'Dear Mother, Father, and Gran'pa! I hope this finds you well as it leaves me. I miss the farm so much and the three of you a lot more than I can say, and, oh, Dugald, too. Hello, postie! Things are going quite all right at the university. It does not seem too hard, except the big books about doctrine and dogmatism often seem more of a study of what men have done rather than what God is doing. I'm not complaining, mind you, just reporting things as you asked me to do." Elspeth stopped reading and glanced up to see how the others were taking all this.

All three had started eating again, and Andrew said as he reached for an oatcake, "It's just an echo of his last week's letter. I'm surprised at the lad. We all know he can write better than that!"

"Just wait until you hear the rest, Andrew, before you judge. 'All the above was written before I went to Balloch, and now I continue this letter a different fellow.' " Bone spoons were set down quietly beside the empty bowls, and each listener pushed his plate aside. Leaning his hand on his chin in anticipation, Gran'pa sighed contentedly. Elspeth had their full attention now. This was more like it. " 'Yes, that last page was written before I met Miss Amelia Godfrey.' "

Dugald could hold his impatience no longer, "Miss Amelia Godfrey! I thought her name was Jean, Jean Irvine, was it no'?"

"His first letter spoke of a Jean somebody; I do believe it *was* Irvine. The feeling I got then was that she would be the one!"

This time Andrew, losing his tolerance, exploded, "Mothers! A young fellow mentions a lassie's name, and they are a'ready speerin' the kirk and namin' the grand we'ans!"

"Aye, Elspeth, lass, will ye not read on?"

" 'Miss Amelia is a preacher lady, an evangelist visiting in Scotland from America. Philadelphia to be exact—not the Philadelphia we read about in the Epistles, Gran'pa! (By the way, Mother, will you send me that book of maps Fraser gave me?) I have never heard a preacher like this woman or a service like hers. Goin' to kirk all my days, I never heard the Word expounded as it was today, not even by Fraser at his best.' "

This brought a gasp from Dugald, and the other men looked askance at the reader. All present knew that Fraser Clegg had been a lot more than a hero of the hour for Bruce. In fact the lad had almost worshiped at his feet before the advent of Bouregarde Gallagher. This woman must indeed be something extraordinary.

Elspeth continued: " 'Mr. Bennett—I'd better tell you about him—is the one who invited me to come to the service; it was to be held in the big front room of the King's Head Inn, in Balmaha, where Peter and I stayed the night on our hiking expedition. The meeting (as they call it) started out ordinary enough, although the singing seemed cheerier right from the beginning. Then Mr. Bennett welcomed everybody before he introduced Miss Amelia. (She said that's what we should call her.) Everybody stood up when she came in, but I was so surprised I just sat on like a big sumph. Then she began to talk. For the next two hours I thought she talked for me alone, but I learned later that is one of her gifts, to have all her listeners think that. Her message was about Philip in the Acts—not the Apostle but the deacon. After reading from the Book of Joel about the Lord's Spirit being poured out on all flesh and the servants and handmaidens being used of God for evangelism, she said her vision from God was to be a Philip. She told how he brought the message of the Gospel to the cities and how those cities were filled with joy. We knew exactly what she meant, because by then we, too, felt that joy. She explained how all those who listened to Philip "paid heed" (it's all in chapter 8) and how they were rewarded with miracles and wonders and signs from God. After she sat down, Mr. Bennett led the whole room in singing. The songs, although the words were the same, had different tunes, and Mr. Bennett made us laugh when he said how he agreed with the Salvationists when they asked, "Why should the devil have all the good tunes?" Then it was prayer time, and I felt more at home with that as it reminded me of our prayers at the farm with Father and Gran'pa and Mam, the way you all just talk with the Lord.' " At that the listeners exchanged happy smiles, replacing the rather anxious looks that had been passing between them during the recital.

"There's more yet! 'After the prayer time, there was a long silence in the room. Nobody moved or spoke, and then finally Miss Amelia said, "A young man here, he is God's man, and he will do great exploits, but for now he is being prepared. We will pray for him, anointing and setting him aside. He is already marked for Jesus, but we are instructed by the Holy Spirit to set a seal on this!" I looked round to see who she meant, but I found all eyes in the room were on me. It was me she meant! Oh, Mam!' "

Elspeth looked up once more, all pretense at hiding her pride in her son vanishing in her secret smile. " 'I had no doubt it was the presence of the Living God in that room, and it all happened just the way she said. Mr. Bennett produced a wee flask of oil, and she put a drop on her finger. The others all gathered about me, and the men laid hands on me while she anointed me with the oil. The rest of the meeting was lost to me, except that I could hear men and women praising the Lord as some were healed of disease. One man who had been deaf could now hear.

" 'The whole thing ended with Mr. Bennett and the party insisting on taking Peter and me back to Glasgow in his huge carriage—it's more like a fancy Gypsy caravan—that he uses to transport the team about the country. Miss Amelia made a joke about Philip, saying that God has not seen fit to transport her in quite the same style as he used for Philip to the Ethiopian yet, but that Mr. Bennett's carriage was the next best thing. They took us right to the end of George Street, and we were still in time for tea at the boardinghouse. Things seem to have settled down here, too, as Mrs. MacIntyre was at her place, pouring the tea, and Miss Jean Irvine is again helping to serve.

" 'I must draw to a close now, as these two days away have put me behind in my studying, so I have about thirty pages to read before I can get to sleep.

" 'My best regards to all my friends at Aribaig. I'm glad you have a new dog. Naming him *Melancholy* is a masterpiece of genius on your part, Mam. Good night and God bless. Your son and grandson, Bruce MacAlister.' "

The grandfather clock showered them with sound as it struck two chimes, breaking the silence.

"My, it was a grand letter. The Lord has him in His hand!"

"Yes, and I do believe we will not have too many exciting things for a while, as the lady told him. God does things decently and in order!"

"Aye, thon sheep must be wonderin' if we've a' gone tae America. They'll be startin' tae eat each other's wool if we dinna hurry up."

Dugald was off across the footbridge before the others reached the doorstep.

Intent on the business of the farm, the other two almost missed Elspeth's parting remarks, "That's all well and good, but I'm most concerned about that Jean. It's the way he writes her name!" For a moment the men looked at each other in amazement; then both started to laugh at the "dite" ways of women. Andrew gently closed the door. "Dite," maybe, but nice to have about the place.

Before they reached the sheep pen, Andrew caught hold of Gran'pa's elbow, "Are they some kind o' Chartists or Shakers, do you think, Bruce?"

"I dinna ken, Andrew, and I dinna fear for him either. The Lord has our lad well in hand all right, and we ken He uses all kinds o' folk for the Plan."

"Aye, but the lad is so innocent. I feel whiles that we sent him out as a lamb among wolves." Reaching into the fold, he picked up a lamb for inspection, and as if to prove his words the mother ewe began making loud noises of protest. Andrew laughed.

"Right you are. I'll say no more. Gran'pa, you're deep in thought. What else have you to say?"

"Just that the Lord Himself was sent oot as a lamb to the slaughter. But to meet a wolf, Bruce didna' need to go to

Glasgow. We've had the real kind right on the doorstep, mind. No, we'll not be anxious for Bruce. It seems to me that between yon Dr. Alexander, at the university, he telt us aboot, and now this Quaker woman, the young fellow is to have a good mixture in his education. He'll turn out fine, never fear! Now we maun get on wi' the shearin', or nane o' us'll have food or a shirt for the winter."

Andrew did not smile this time.

⊸⊷{ 13 }⊶⊷⊸

"Y ou're lookin' 'fair sonsy,' as my father would say in his best professional manner. The highlands must be improving weatherwise, or did you go to the Riviera to get that brown?" The friends laughed heartily at the joke. Peter was in a high mood.

Bruce replied with a sideways look at the other, "You look all right yourself, Dr. Peter Blair. You're the one who went to France, you rascal, and for a whole year, too! I missed your noisy presence about the place here." Since he had left to begin his internship at the infirmary, Peter's old room at the end of the corridor had remained vacant, until two weeks ago.

"Believe you me, yon was no Grand Tour of the Riviera but was a working, tramping expedition to get material for my thesis, as you very well know. What you don't know is that I've decided to go in for social reform. As I am now considered a doctor, that might seem a bit funny to some folk, including yourself, but Father agrees with me about my plans. I had to do a deal of talking, first, but he ended up by saying if that is truly what I want, then I'll have his unholy blessing." All trace of banter left as Peter finished speaking. Bruce smiled secretly as he visualized the scene of agreement between father and son. Having spent a fortnight at the sprawling Blair home in Burntisland, while convalescing from a bout of pleurisy, as well as visiting several weekends, Bruce knew this happy-go-lucky household to be as different from the farm in Aribaig as "chalk from cheese," as Dugald would say. Peter's father, an older and slightly larger edition of Peter, could be considered the typical Scottish physician. Not until Bruce MacAlister's third visit did he discover the Blair family's pathetically guarded secret: The good doctor had an overfondness for the bottle. Once only did Peter allude to it—and then obscurely.

"Father has a recurring ailment. Every ten weeks or so this weakness attacks him, and we just have to weather it through. About four days it lasts, and Dr. Pettigrew takes care of his patients for that time!" Gazing directly into Bruce's face as he spoke, he dared him to contradict those words. Bruce responded with a brief touch of hand to shoulder before sadly turning away. Following this exchange, Bruce never forgot to pray for Dr. Blair, this good, kind man, a self-professed athiest, whose need was so great.

Peter brought him back to the present with a snap of his fingers. "Sorry, Peter, old chap, what was that you said?"

"You're dreaming about Jean again, no doubt. Never mind, I only asked what you yourself have been up to since I saw you. If you missed your chances to talk with the Bonnie Jean 'in private,' then you're less of a man than I thought!" The telltale flags of color rushed to Bruce's cheeks, and now his prayer was that soon he would surely be mature enough to stop blushing.

"As a matter of fact, and for your information, Miss Jean Irvine spent all last summer in Yorkshire. After that Granny Mac took her to London for the 'season,' whatever that means, and as she only returned to Strathcona House for her parents' arrival from India, a fortnight ago, I've hardly seen her since you left." Peter yawned, unimpressed by the long explanation.

"You know all her doings, anyway. That tells me a lot."

Exasperated, Bruce retorted, "As for me, I was too busy being inaugurated into the realm of field ministry here in the slums and tenements of this not-so-fair city to bother about anything else—the most unromantic Gorbals to be exact. My, it's a cesspool. You should have been here yourself and seen it. You don't need to go to France for that kind of expedition. I received another kind of education in what the ravages of the demon drink can do, but when you try to see. . . ."

"I suppose you've some kind of holy answer for that, too. Well, let me tell you this: The circumstances are not always the reason, at least not on the surface. You preachers think you have it all cut and dried, but I have my own ideas. Understand the causes behind the drinking before you make your judgment! The miserable existence endured by most of your tenement dwellers is one reason, I admit, but I tell you, man, poverty's not the only reason. A man can have all one body could need and still indulge to the furthest extremes!" Astonishment registered on Bruce's face as he stared at a completely transformed Peter.

"Peter, I'm sorry if what I said upset you, but there's something else bothering you, I know. Can you not let me help you?"

"Oh, will you just leave me alone? I'm not interested in your holy theories. Come back when things are evened out more fair like and tell me about your God. In the meantime I'll be on the side of social reform and helping individuals from the point of view of those who say we are only what we make ourselves."

"You contradict yourself, and so do they. If we are only what we make ourselves, how did we spring out of mud or monkeys? Did we plan that?"

"Now you're twistin' my words. I'm sorry, man, we shouldna' argue. I don't suppose it will ever be reconciled. Tell me about Aribaig. How are your grandfather and Dugald? Does the postie still read your letters before they're opened? What of your parents? And Melancholy of course!" The questions came thick and fast, as if Peter wanted to forget his outburst, as indeed he did. Bruce began to relate stories of his weeks at Aribaig when he worked from dawn to dark, garnering for last winter. Hay and harvest, cattle sales and sheep shearing, his report was good and filled with shared jokes. Both laughed out loud when he related Dugald's half-hearted attempts to help with putting up the new tiled roof to replace the worn-out thatch.

"Dugald surely thinks being a 'man of letters' means a postman."

"And, now that you're up-to-date with my news and are assured that the MacAlister fortunes are secure for one more year at least, tell me about Burntisland and Dr. Pettigrew."

"Old Pettifog is fine; why ask me? Oh, now I remember. He didna care for your particular brand of Christianity, did he? It seems to me that he and your "Angry Angus"—oh, I know you never complained much, but I'm a doctor, remember, and that makes me a champion guesser, too—would get on fine together! We'd best not start into that subject again. We had no need for Petti's help till now, and that only because Father is here for the celebration of my accomplishments. No bouts for quite a while, I'm glad to report."

Glancing at Bruce, before the faraway look could return to that sensitive face he continued, "But you know, if we're not to be late for Mrs. MacIntyre's spring soiree—and you do want to make a good first impression on Bonnie Jean's 'pukka sahib' parents, don't you?—we'd better hurry up. As usual you look every inch the highland laird in that kilt. I wish I could wear one, but my knees. . . . Oh, well, you can't have everything, it seems, and my brain makes up for my brawn!"

Laughing again, they made their way to the staircase, but Peter's remarks served to remind Bruce of the coming ordeal, bringing the blush to his face again. The annual event at Strathcona House would mark many changes this year, the end of Bruce's fourth and final term at the university being one. Thinking of it brought his mind round to the news item quoted by Gran'pa in last week's letter. It was an article in the *Inverness Times* that read, "Finally, after 400 years of existence, Glasgow's Kelvinside University is given authority to grant the degree doctor of divinity."

Previously those candidates deserving of that honor had to spend a term at Oxford or Saint Andrews. He would not mention it to Peter until he was sure himself, but he would tell Mrs. MacIntyre, and she would tell Jean.

Suddenly, his natural high spirits and good humor restored, the new doctor began to sing, urging Bruce to join in. "Here come the tattie howkers, who saw the tattie howkers? Here come the tattie howkers, down fae the glen!"

Hearing them, Beulah MacIntyre smiled indulgently. The mouse, Penelope, always came to her mind when she saw Peter, even after four years. She still had a secret soft spot for each of these young men. Now they stopped at the drawing-room door, composing their faces with an unconvincing display of seriousness before making their entrance.

The MacIntyre house was full to overflowing. Although happy to welcome her daughter, Jessica, and her husband, Cameron, home from India, Beulah still found it difficult to adjust to all the changes involved. She pondered the accommodations for the Irvine retinue. No other word quite described them, as the group included two native servants, brought "home" for convenience' sake, as far as Cameron was concerned, but really not too convenient for the others in the house.

They had been home for a fortnight, and Cameron was becoming restless. Tonight's celebration would only be another of Mother-in-law's interminable dry soirees, to be tolerated for his wife's sake. That Beulah had sacrificed her little private sitting room to give the couple breathing space he counted only as his due. The couple were there now, preparing for the party.

The tone in her voice told him that as usual Jessica was making plans. "Cameron, I know this is difficult for you, but if you could just be patient a wee while longer. After all, Jean is our one and only, and she did receive a teacher's certificate with extra mention for English composition, and—"

"Be patient, you say! *Be patient!* I'd like to know what you think I've been doing all the time since we arrived? Surrounded by planning, scheming women, no privacy because when we are by ourselves in here, we still have to talk in whispers, dear Mama being just through the wall. Oh, Jessie, my love, I'm sorry! Don't cry like that."

Though she had learned over the years that these lightning mood changes of her husband's were not to be trusted, Jessica still welcomed the moments when he appeared to soften up. Usually when she had the vapors, as he called her bouts of crying, he would simply hold her close, and quite soon she would stop. Not this time though.

After a minute, when she was still crying, he spoke above her head, "What else do you want me to do, Jessie? You know I would do almost anything to stop your crying."

Hiccupping a few times, she began to relate her plan one more time. . . . *Maybe this time* . . . . "So, if we can only stay here for a few more weeks, until things settle down, you can put in for your retirement, and we would never need to return to the Punjab, and Mama would help us get a place of our own, and if Raju and Larissa—"

Cameron pulled away angrily. Forgetting his brief lapse into softness and no longer caring who heard, he let out a roar, "Why are we on about that again? I am not ready to retire for at least four more years, and we've talked all this out before. You know I'm in no hurry to return to this cold, empty land. As for the servants, they will go where we go. They have no choice! This discussion is ridiculous. *No more!* Jean will return to India with us. Back in the Punjab she could have her choice of marriage partners, maybe even a younger son with a title, if you both keep quiet about her so-called education degree."

Jessica began to weep again, this time silently into her handkerchief. She had placed high hopes on manipulating him, but she should have known he could not be swayed that easily. Mama had advised her not to say anything yet. She always wanted everything organized.

Cameron, speaking quietly now, itself a warning signal, said, "You know I can only tolerate so much of your vapors. Enough, I'm away out for a breath of fresh air. I want to hear no more of this, or of your squalling. You and your plans. Keep me out of them! If we were at the club, maybe I could put up with all this, but here no—" The door slammed shut behind him, and Jessica, pressing hard with her hanky, tried to choke back the sobs. If Mama came in now, she would only say, "I told you so." Full of bitter disappointment at the hopelessness of it all, she still knew she would go with him, even in her distress.

"Oh, Cameron! Cameron, what will I do now? Jean doesn't want to go back to India, and neither do I. Raju has asked to stay near her, but then what should I do about Larissa? Oh, what is going to happen to us all?"

Unaware of any of this and wanting only to please her auntie Beulah, who had asked her to help entertain the guests, Faye Felicity Gordon did not know what she might be stirring up when she spoke to Jean's father as he plunged down the garden path.

"Good evening, Colonel Irvine. Lovely evening, isn't it?"

"Humph!"

Faye Felicity was not easily put off, so she tried again. Surely this man should be proud that his daughter had earned her degree as a teacher and extra plaudits for English composition.

"You and Mrs. Irvine must be very proud of Jean's receiving her certificate with honors. And she looks so nice in that bonnie frock you brought from India. I think. . . ." Whatever she thought fell on deaf ears as the colonel went crashing off through the bushes. His angry mutterings about women were not fit for the delicate ears of this prim spinster. Paying not the slightest attention to where he stepped, he failed to see the large figure looming toward him from the opposite direction until he suddenly found himself in a heap on the ground, his limbs sprawled in a most undignified manner with those of some other intruder, fortunately a man.

Before he could extricate himself, the figure spoke, "Correct me if I'm wrong, sir, but I believe you are out here for the same reason as myself." With amazing speed and little to-do, the newcomer righted himself and Colonel Irvine before reaching into an immense jacket pocket to produce a silver flask. Removing the cap with habitual expertise, he kept speaking: "You need a dram. Allow me sir!" Without hesitation the colonel grabbed the silver bottle and gulped, gasping as the potent mouthful stopped his breath.

"Ye are drinking the very best Glenlivet, sir. I'll guarantee it'll put hair on your chest or at least a smile on your face, before you have time to say, 'I thank you'!"

Wiping his mouth with the back of his hand, Cameron said, "Forgive me, please! I forgot my manners, but the truth is I'm so fed up with all the polite piffle-paffle of the women—and most of the men, too! But you, sir, you seem to have some sense, although I have not yet had the honor of your acquaintance."

"My turn to apologize. The name's Blair, Peter Blair, physician and surgeon, at your service. Here to witness my son's launching into the same thankless pursuit of health for the masses, who neither want it nor need it for the most part. . . . Sometimes I think . . . , but never mind. If I start on my opinions on the subject—or most subjects, for that matter—we could be camped out here all night. Am I to guess who you are, or . . . ?"

"Colonel Cameron Irvine, but please, doctor, call me Cam. All my friends at the club in the Punjab—more my home than this, I may add—address me thus. As I already consider yourself as a friend in need, as well as indeed, you must. . . ."

"In that case I insist you call me Blair. I always liked my last name best, so when our first was a boy and my wife wished to call him Peter after me, I took my last name for first. Have another wee mouthful of the Glen. If you've just returned from the Punjab, you must be feeling the chill. Aye, I see you shivering!"

"We arrived a fortnight ago, and I have not yet become accustomed to this terrible climate or to the refreshments. Yes, I will indulge in another drop. As you may know, tea is one of the main reasons we are all in India, but it never did become my favorite beverage. I must say, Blair, old man, this is the best whiskey I've ever tasted, even better than what the club had to offer!" as he spoke he upended the flask and drained it. Undaunted, his new friend reached again into the deep recesses of his coat to provide, this time, not a flask, but a flat bottle. Without ceremony, he drank deeply from it. Their mutual maudlin admiration might have continued indefinitely, except for Faye Felicity.

Hidden from the two men, she had witnessed the whole encounter. After she assured herself the colonel was not hurt, she hoped they would soon move. As time passed and she began to feel chilled, she decided to return to the house. Soon the sounds of their hilarious laughter reached her, the sound reminding her of many Saturday nights spent at the London Missionary Society mission hall, when the derelict drunks gathered to be given a bed and food. Reaching the merrymakers, she confirmed her earlier suspicion that the two were actually still seated on the ground, blithely heedless of the dampness or the fact that they occupied all the pathway between the rosebushes on one side and the raspberry canes on the other.

Her tone betrayed shocked embarrassment as she said their names, "Dr. Blair and Colonel Irvine?"

"Yes, my dear, and what can we do for you? Would you care to join us in a little drink? Move over, Cam!"

Their sodden laughter rang out again. Having consumed the contents of both flask and bottle, they were far beyond caring about appearances. Momentarily at a loss, Faye stood looking down at the revelers. Dr. Blair continued, "Well! Well! If it isn't Miss Charity herself. Faith, hope, and charity, you know? But the greatest of these is charity. You see, I know my Bible!" This remark sparked the roisterers into fresh peals of hysterical merriment. At least, to Faye's professional ears, Colonel Irvine was certainly hysterical. Abruptly the colonel stopped laughing. Dr. Blair, more in control than his new friend, leaned close to catch the mumbled words. Instead of words he heard sobs, and before he could offer consolation of any kind, the "friend" ungratefully emptied the contents of his stomach without care of direction. Instantly sobered, Blair bellowed out an oath, and immediately the whole scene assumed the characteristics of a vaudeville play for the next few minutes. Without hesitation, Faye Felicity stepped in to take control of the situation.

14

Faye's natural common sense, along with her experiences in the mission came to the fore. Quickly she propelled the limp man toward the water pump at the bottom of the garden. Without ceremony she held his head under, indicating to Dr. Blair, who had followed them, to crank the pump handle. The doctor, shamefaced but ever eloquent, even in this emergency, was still talking.

"I must apologize for all this, Miss Gordon. My fault entirely! I trust you will find it in your heart to forgive and forget?"

Using the edge of her shawl to wipe the colonel's head, Faye answered curtly, "I won't speak of this to our hostess, if that's what you mean. Further I will not promise!" Blair started to babble his thanks, but she cut him off: "Hush, I hear someone coming!"

"Curse it! The place is becoming a regular Broomielaw on a Saturday afternoon!" The doctor continued to mutter sourly to himself. Cameron, leaning in a most ungainly fashion on Faye's shoulder, seemed oblivious to his circumstances. The footsteps came closer. Now they could hear disembodied voices moving in the direction of the summerhouse. Into full view, and completely unaware of being under scrutiny, stepped the evening's guest of honor and, walking suspiciously close beside Jean, decked in all his finery, came the kilted highlander, Bruce MacAlister.

*　　　*　　　*

Bruce was dizzy with joy—not for him the imitation delights of an alcoholic daze. After adoring Jean Irvine from a distance for four years and being content with a shy smile and a glance from lowered lashes once in a while, too busy to try for more, he now felt himself transported. Gravitating toward her, away from the party crowd, and hardly daring to imagine her response, he had suggested they walk in the garden.

Indoors had suddenly become stifling to Bruce and, he guessed, to Jean as well. Treading the dark path between the congested bushes, he dredged up some more courage and reached out to take her hand as she stumbled slightly. She allowed it to remain, and his cup ran over. During the course of the evening, he had entered wholeheartedly into the festivities, rejoicing with his friend Peter, as well as the young woman by his side at the moment, for their achievements. His confidence building up with each step, he exulted. Here, close beside him, walked Jean Irvine. Bruce did not understand how he knew, but somehow he had recognized from the first, even as he tried to escape the knowledge, that someday she would be his own, his one and only love.

Engrossed in each other and oblivious to tne stealthy figures close by, the couple passed within a few feet of the old pump and stopped. Then, in one accord and without further words they walked together up the steps leading up to the old summerhouse.

"Jean, I mean Miss Irvine!" Her laugh rang out in the still air of the garden and carried clearly to the three unwilling listeners. If Bruce was exultant, Jean was equally so.

"We'll dispense with formalities shall we? . . . Bruce!" the last word shy in spite of the brave beginning.

"Yes, oh, yes! Call me Bruce. I love you!" The unhappy watchers, frozen now with embarrassment, dared not glance at one another. Faye Felicity wondered how long they could remain undetected. Suddenly Cameron Irvine shook himself free of Blair and Faye and leaped into action. The movement brought a measure of sobriety. Picking up a stray raspberry cane from the ground, he quickly reached the summerhouse. The scene would have been comic were it not so pathetic. Unable to stop his headlong dash, Faye Felicity and Blair could only follow the would-be avenger.

"By Jove, this has gone far enough. Unhand my daughter, you scoundrel!"

Bruce came out of his bemused state instantly as the noises, heard vaguely in the background, erupted beside him. Before he could turn round, a rough hand seized his jacket, and his reaction was automatic. Swinging with clenched fist, Bruce caught the attacker full in the face with a powerful blow. At once the summerhouse filled with people, all in frenzied action.

Jean was screaming, "You've killed him! You've killed my father!" Her father, now flat on his back on the ground, did indeed appear to be dead. From the shadowed garden ran Jessica, closely followed by the two Indian servants. Seeing her husband prostrate, after hearing Jean's hysterical cry she promptly fainted. Raju caught her before she fell.

Recounting it all to his son, later, Dr. Blair could hardly contain his glee. "It was like the circus, son, but that female, what's her name again? Och yes, Faye, took charge of the whole matter. She sent the servant girl for more water; then she rushed over to young Jean, who was still hysterical.

" 'You've killed my father, he's dead. You killed him!' she screamed at the poor fish. Of course the colonel was far from dead, just plastered, but only I knew that so far. Or no, maybe the female had the sense to know it, too. Anyway instead of comforting young Jean, she slapped her. A wonderful cure for hysteria and being used more all the time, I hear. If they'd asked me, I would have told them about it years ago. Seeing my amusement, this Faye then turned on me with her orders if you please.

" 'You, sir,' she said to me. 'A physician, I believe?'

" 'That I am indeed,' I answered, prepared to render my pedigree, if need be, but she cut in again.

" 'Then please examine Colonel Irvine before we have him carried into the house. I fear some bones may be broken, and we do not want to move him, should that be the case.' I found myself obeying without question." Peter almost grinned at that, but the situation had taken a serious turn, and poor Bruce would be the worst sufferer. Where had the overconscientious fool gotten to?

His own first inkling that something was amiss came when the procession began. First Jean and the Indian servant girl led a still-fainting Mrs. Irvine through the doorway. Next came his father and the manservant, Raju, carrying the colonel and being directed by the "female," as his father referred to Faye Felicity.

At that point Mrs. MacIntyre appeared out of the crowd of guests and signaled to Peter. When he reached her side, she whispered crisply in his ear, "Mr. Blair, please be so kind as to direct the guests to the next part of the evening's entertainment. Then instruct Betsy to start serving the buffet. I'll be much obliged to you!" Bemused by the request and amazed at the whole turn of events, a speechless Peter hurried to obey, all the time wondering where his friend was. Surely what was slowly creeping into his mind could not be true. Och, no! The highland laddie had more sense, or did he? The fellow was in love and. . . . Soon most of the group, crowded in the hallway to watch, were eating out of his hand as he went into his clown act. It was some time later before he thought of Bruce again. By then Bruce had disappeared!

Even as his clenched fist found contact with the face of his attacker, Bruce regretted his action. But it was too late. The heavy thud of a body hitting the floorboards of the summer-house, followed by the scream from Jean, immobilized him for just a second. Then the rush of people coming from all directions further confused him. Looking round quickly he saw Peter's father. Dr. Blair caught his arm.

"He'll be all right, my boy, never you fear, but I think you better make yourself scarce for a while!" Bruce needed no second urging. What had been, a few minutes before, an idyllic setting for a scene of youthful romance had turned into a horrific nightmare. Taking the back way, for this moment free of guests and servants, he ran for the stairs. Seconds later he was making his way along George Street, carrying the carelessly bundled up pack containing his one remaining suit of home-spuns and his Bible. None noticed him leave.

Glasgow's Central Station was almost deserted. The kiosks and newsstands, denuded of their wares, reminded Bruce, appropriately enough in his present mood, of the graveyard in Aribaig. Thinking of home brought a tightening to his throat, but he forced it back.

Even such longing for his home was as nothing to the sadness he felt now for what he had just forfeited. Lifting his head up, he felt himself droop with tiredness and dejection. Never again to hear Jean speak his name in that special way she had tonight for the first time. Shy and sweet yet sure. Instead, the echo of her scream resounded through his head, filling him with renewed horror: "You've killed my father!"

Groaning aloud, he bent himself double across the waiting-room table. Leaning his head on his hands, he remained unaware of any other presence until someone spoke above him. An aged porter, armed with a long-handled broom, which he moved with little concentration or interest across the waiting-room floor, paused in his work to gaze at the kilted man.

Nodding wisely, accustomed to watching the endless currents of humanity ebbing and flowing daily and leaving jetsam of every kind, the old man swished his way round Bruce. Earlier he had answered the young man's question about the next train to Fort William, but he sensed something deeper here. The students from the university—and Benny Stout didn't need to be told who were students—usually came in droves to leap on a train just as it was pulling away from the platform, loaded down with boxes full of heavy books and other paraphernalia. This one had only a small homespun bundle, and besides, he was too early altogether. By Benny's counting the university didn't get out for about another six weeks. Then for about three days after that, the station would be crowded with students going off to only God knew what or where.

Unable to contain his curiosity longer, Benny spoke, "Like A said before, nae trains till the morrow for Fort William. Are ye goin' tae sit here til' then?"

"Eh, what? Oh, no! I'm just trying to make up my mind what to do till then. I can't go back. . . ." His mouth filled with bitter-tasting bile at the memory of the past two hours, but even that could not hide the soft sound of his highland brogue. "Sorry if I'm disturbing you, sir!"

Benny laughed. "Dinna call me sir, and ye're no' disturbin' me. It's time for my tea. Come away in to the bothy, and I'll gie ye a cup." Refusal hovered on Bruce's lips, but catching a glimpse of something on the porter's face, he decided to accept the kind offer.

Once started, Benny kept chattering. The tea, hot and strong and sweet, calmed the storm within Bruce, and he began to take in his surroundings. An immense coal fire burned in the grate, and even if the chair upon which he sat was hard, Bruce felt himself slipping off to sleep in spite of everything. A sudden silence in the warm bothy struck him. Then Benny asked another question, "Have ye nae place to go and wait then?"

"Oh, yes! I mean, not exactly. There are a few places I could go, were it not the middle of the night. But don't bother about me. I thank you for the tea and your concern but—" In his haste to be off, he jumped to his feet, dropping his bundle. The flimsy string broke, and the bundle flew open, revealing his pathetic little pile of belongings and his Bible. As both men bent to pick it up hand touched hand, and immediately both became aware of a change in the atmosphere.

"It's a divinity student ye are then?" Benny had picked up the Bible and held it out to Bruce as he spoke.

"I was one, yes! But after what happened tonight, I don't know if I'll be able to finish!" He took a deep breath, "Don't let me keep you from your work, sir."

"I tell't ye no' tae call me sir! Just call me Benny."

"Thank you, Benny. I'll be on my way now!"

"What's your hurry, if you have till mornin' to catch yer train? No, I'm thinkin ye'll need a place tae sleep and a bit breakfast, before ye get on the Fort William train. Mysel' now, I dinna feenish ma shift 'til six o'clock. I ken what we'll do! Ye see thon curtain? Well, it hides a cot bed for the porters on the split shift. Ye can sleep there while A feenish ma shift, and then I'll take ye tae my friend Mr. George Bennett!"

"Bruce MacAlister, am I to understand you correctly when you say you don't intend to finish at the university because of a fight of some kind, or have I somehow missed the point?" Mr. George Bennett frowned in concentration as he asked the question. The two were seated on opposite sides of the small breakfast table in Mr. Bennett's morning room. The housekeeper had just wheeled in a trolley of steaming hot plates, and even before she had time to remove the covers, the tantalizing smell of bacon and eggs assailed their nostrils.

"Not just a fight of some kind, Mr. Bennett. I brutally swung with all my force to hit a man full in the face. . . . A man not in full possession of his faculties and certainly not very strong. Why, when I earlier caught a glimpse of Colonel Irvine, although I still have not been introduced to the gentleman, I thought his coloring very bad. My friend Peter, who is now a doctor, even mentioned the word *jaundiced*. The last I saw of him—the colonel, I mean—he looked like a corpse strung out on the summerhouse boards. Oh, my lord!"

"I have many questions about all this. First, I am surprised that you ran from your responsibility there. Next, would the fine colonel, by any chance, have been consuming alcohol before he rushed in to attack you? Because I've heard of the "pukka sahibs." They live on spiritous liquors, and in that climate especially, it sends them out of their heads."

"Dr. Blair it was who said I should make myself scarce, and he would take care of everything. Jean's face, too, and her terrible, frightened screaming made me rush away. I will not make excuses. The colonel was protecting his daughter as he saw fit, and he had every right to do that. About the spirits, yes, I could smell them, but as you say, the men on furlough from India all seem to imbibe quite a bit. I have heard, too, it is because of the bad water in that land and—"

"You won't make excuses for yourself, but you will make them for the colonel. Oh, well, we must not judge. You know of course that I'm acquainted with Mrs. MacIntyre, although our paths have not crossed that often. After I met with yourself and young Peter at Mr. Taggert's inn, she sent me a nice letter of thanks and an invitation. I had caught a bad case of rheumatism in Balmaha, and by the time I had recovered sufficiently to be sociable, we had to leave for Philadelphia, where, as you know, we spent the next two years. So I never was able to accept that invitation. I remember Mrs. MacIntyre as a most strong-minded lady. But about your present predicament, it is not even to be considered that you give up your university work when you are so close to your goal. I do see where it might not be expedient for you to stay at Strathcona House under the circumstances, so you'll stay here, with me. Oh, I'll not listen to your arguments!" he cried as Bruce made a sound of protest. "When you go to your classes on Monday, I'll pay a visit to Mrs. MacIntyre and get the rights of it all."

"Final-year divinity students must have exemplary behavior. When he hears about this, Professor Alexander will have me expelled at once."

"Who is going to tell the professor? Not Colonel Irvine. If he was as far-gone in spirits as I suspect, he won't be remembering much; and if he does remember, it will be with shame, and he'll tell no one else. His family, too, will not wish it to be talked about anywhere. Who else witnessed it? Your friend Peter is an astute young man, as I recall. He won't tell. His father? If your assailant became his patient, medical ethics will keep him silent. Who else did you say was there?"

"Miss Faye Felicity Gordon, I'm sure she saw everything!" George Bennett looked closely at Bruce as his youthful visitor groaned again, head on hands, almost in an attitude of prayer. So serious, so dedicated and real. Truly an anointed one, and George Bennett held no doubt whatsoever that God had arranged the meeting with Benny at the station, Benny being a deacon from their assembly. They both had a part in this drama. To George Bennett it seemed a storm in a teacup compared to some of the tragic happenings he had witnessed during his own sixty-five years of serving the Lord, but it was a terribly serious business to his young friend and as such must not be treated lightly.

"That's settled then! There'll be no more talk of entraining for Fort William until you have your papers. I'll arrange for everything, and I'll find out all you'll want to know about the situation at Strathcona House."

During their discussion Bruce had realized how his hasty retreat must appear to Jean and Peter. Knowing himself not to be a coward, he could not understand how his feelings of being unable to face them could confront him. Face them he must, but not today. The wisdom of Mr. Bennett's plan was evident; it was not so much fear that filled him but a reluctance to face the scorn of his newly discovered love. He could never pay her court now, after striking her father down.

Mr. Bennett was speaking again, "Nothing to be gained by your starving yourself, either; eat up some of this good food, or Mrs. Oliver will be offended. Then what about coming to meeting with me? It is still Sunday, you know."

15

No one, not even her beloved Jean or her spiritual daughter Faye Felicity, ever discovered exactly what passed between George Bennett and Beulah MacIntyre that day. Betsy related the story to Cook over their bedtime cup of tea.

"The gentleman came to the door, and when I told him Mrs. MacIntyre was not 'at home,' he just stood there, waiting. When I told him again that the mistress was not receiving visitors, he asked for Miss Jean, and I must say I was shocked at his cheek. I told him Miss Jean was not 'at home' either. I would have slammed the door in his face, if he hadn't put his foot in it! My but these are good scones, Cook. I think I will have another one."

"Then what happened, Betsy?" Rising to refill the teapot, Cook glanced back over her shoulder to hear the best part.

"He smiled at me and said, awful nicelike, 'Then I'll wait until one of them is at home!' I don't know what I would've done if the mistress herself had no' come up behind me and invited him in. As you know, she took him to her private sitting room, and they were there together until the tea gong. She never even ordered tea or anything!"

Beulah had actually asked her visitor to stay to tea, but he had declined politely, "Thank you, no, madam, this being meeting night, and I'm obliged to attend, especially as I missed this morning."

"You missed meeting! Why, Mr. Bennett, I'm surprised."

"Yes, I attended kirk with young MacAlister, instead. I'll be going now then, Mistress MacIntyre, and trust you to take care of all the matters we discussed."

"You may trust me indeed, Mr. Bennett. Good evening to you!"

George Bennett's decision not to delay his visit to Strathcona House until Monday had come after he had returned from the service. Bruce had been assigned a room and sent there to rest. Wishing to assure himself that his young guest was indeed resting, George quietly pushed open the door of the room, to find Bruce on his knees and literally crying out to God, "I'm sorry, Lord! I see now where I should not have told Jean about loving her. I should never have presumed to ask her to walk out with me. No wonder Your wrath was turned on me. As a penance I'll not look at her or any woman, ever again. From now on, I take an—"

Before he could say more, George announced his presence as he called out, "Don't swear an oath or a vow. Don't even think of it until you have calmed down sufficiently to have rational thoughts. I've brought a potion for you. You'll oblige me by swallowing it now and saying no more of this swearing until you wake up." Reluctantly Bruce obeyed his benefactor and indeed as soon as he swallowed the potion was immediately asleep.

Waking refreshed and finding George almost jubilant, following his private interview with Mrs. MacIntyre, Bruce was incredulous. "You mean Mistress MacIntyre, the same Mistress MacIntyre, said all *that*?"

"You grieve me, Bruce, implying I speak untruth. Mrs. MacIntyre did indeed say it. For the present, however, it will be expedient for us to keep these matters to ourselves. She says, and I can only agree, the more I think on it, that you rushed your suit. I realize you've known Jean for four years, but still and all. . . .Our advice, for the time being anyway, is this: You will wait out your time at the university here, quietly and productively, so you'll finish your term and get your ordination. You can write to your parents, telling them you've moved in with me. No further explanation is required than the truth. Strathcona House is crowded. Now, if we hurry up, we'll not arrive too late for meeting."

The singing was well under way when the two walked into the meeting hall. Glancing round the poorly built structure, water stains showing plainly through the whitewash, Bruce felt strange. He stood politely beside his benefactor, and soon the first feeling of unease began to wear off as he noted the deep sincerity on the rapt faces of the congregation. Determined not to get too involved with his emotions, he deliberately set his mind to analyze from a safe distance. Soon he found himself comparing this simple worship service to a grand lecture, given in splendid rhetoric, by the great Dr. Alexander only last week, on the dangers of allowing feelings to overcome logic and common sense.

From the corner of his eye he watched Mr. Bennett lifting up his hands as the crowd sang what sounded to Bruce like the words of Psalm 25, but surely it could not be; the tune was so lively. An excited older woman was sweating it out on the old rattletrap of a piano, and yes, sure enough, there was a girl shaking a tambourine. Caught between the discomfort of unfamiliar surroundings and the desire to please his host, Bruce could only stand and wonder if all this excitement could really be an insult to the Almighty, or if it could be pleasing in His sight, as the man who had just finished speaking had prayed. They all seemed so genuine, yet according to Dr. Alexander, the dignity of worship must be maintained at all times. As if in reply to his unspoken thoughts, the noise faded to a hush. The dingy hall was transformed. Bruce gazed, awestruck, as the drab walls began to glow with an opalescent shimmering like silver raindrops in a summer evening shower.

Into the silence George Bennett's voice penetrated as he whispered reverently, "It's the shekinah glory! Remove your shoes, you are on holy ground." Without question the members of this strange congregation moved as one, and Bruce found himself untying his shoelaces with the others, a desire to obey, far removed from his natural inclination, compelling him.

"Realizing that the Holy Bible is our ultimate text, it still behooves us to put it aside while we speak of the pressures of the moment, for instance, your upcoming final examinations and the eventual emergence upon a world already awaiting in breathless expectation for your initial homily, which will, no doubt, render your hearers euphoric with pious admiration!" Although Dr. Alexander addressed his class of twenty or so graduating hopefuls, his high-sounding remarks were aimed specifically at only one: Bruce MacAlister. Polite laughter rippled round the lofty room, but for the most part the young men present were not amused. "Angry Angus" had long since outplayed this audience, and now his darts of satiric humor, aimed at Bruce, failed to stir them. Seeing in Bruce, from their first encounter, the person he himself wished to be but could not be had infuriated him to the point where he could no longer think rationally where Bruce was concerned—rather the opposite. Indeed this man, teacher of preachers and weeder of chaff from the real grain, had within him a root of bitterness blinding him from obvious truth and stemming from his own lost zeal. Throughout the four years of training and pruning the group facing him now, he had sometimes, with a brutality he had not known he possessed, baited the younger man without mercy, calling it chastening and telling himself with trite justification how his methods would prove whether or not MacAlister had true grit.

Today, as on that far-off first day in this very room, Bruce sat on his bench, oblivious not only to the professor but to his complete surroundings while his mind and heart wandered. Having completed the assigned Bible test, he had turned the pages to Psalm 150, deciding to use the remaining time, which he considered free, to ponder the meaning of the words. His thoughts returned to Sunday night's meeting with Mr. Bennett's group of believers. The speaker's "key note," what they had been taught must be included in all their sermons, had been "the joy of praise." This rankled. Could it be true that God took pleasure in such crudity? That He was honored by humble folk, like the piano thumper sweating away on her stool and the tuneless rattlings of the tambourine shaker? Or was Dr. Alexander right in maintaining that only the sounds from high, lofty pipe organs and the slow, dignified renditions of the words of the Psalter would be acceptable to the Lord?

The angry swish of the rod jerked Bruce out of his reverie. Instinctively he ducked his head, while snapping shut the treasured Bible. Waves of indescribable pain ripped into Bruce as the cruel lash bit his unprotected hand. Immediately a searing red line rose on the flesh. A shocked gasp swept the room. None but Alexander knew that the open Bible itself had been his target. Bruce's hand had moved too quickly to close it, and now it was difficult to tell who had undergone the greatest shock, Bruce or the professor. The expression upon the latter's face appeared comical to the uninitiated. Within the room the echo of the whiplash reverberated in the ensuing silence.

Finally, in an effort to hide his discomfiture, Alexander blustered, "I'm sure our big braw highland chieftain will not allow a wee strap to hinder him, will ye MacAlister?" Bruce shook his head, too bewildered with pain to answer. His hand throbbed, already assuming balloonlike proportions as it began to swell alarmingly. "Away to the infirmary wi' ye then, ye big lassie, and don't let me see ye in class again the day!"

Surprised at the unexpected and unusual note of gentleness cloaked within the rough words, Bruce gladly obeyed.

Walking back down the corridor, after receiving peremptory instructions not to use the hand for at least a week, Bruce let his mind return to his earlier questing. This time he added a personal inquiry: "Why, God, if You are so interested in each person's doings, has such an occurrence been allowed to happen to me at such a time as this, when I am so soon to be officially dedicated into Your service?" His right hand would certainly be out of commission for a while. Even if he had no intention of obeying the crabbit old martinet of a nursing sister who had bandaged his hand, he still knew the injury could hamper him.

But surely it would not be enough to obstruct his goal! He remembered what Gran'pa would say, if he were here now, "The de'il meant it for evil, but God will turn it for good!" Thoughts of home brought a faint smile to his lips as he passed the corner and turned toward the doorway of the infirmary.

The solitary figure waiting at the end of the corridor, witnessed that shaky smile. Full of secret remorse and concern, which he would have died rather than admit or show, Professor Alexander tried to reassure himself that Bruce would indeed be able to complete his examinations. Then he hurried away to continue his own bitter questing, before anyone could see him there.

The minute the evening meal was cleared away and Mrs. Oliver had clucked over his disfigured hand, now assuming strange colors and dimensions although the pain seemed easier, Bruce started on his final essay, setting aside the small packet of powders pressed upon him by Mr. Bennett to lessen the pain. He would swallow one at bedtime, if he still needed to. Gritting his teeth, he bent to the task.

Seated in a tight row outside the massive doors leading to the awesome and rather frightening hall of divinity, ten students waited in solemn silence. Among them sat Bruce MacAlister.

Ten pairs of eyes trained on the great brass door handles, waiting for them to twist upward. Then a page boy, bearing the tidings of they knew not what, would enter, and it would all be over. Whatever happened from this moment on was completely beyond their control.

Earlier, one by one the acolytes had disappeared behind that door, entering into the austere presence of the final examining board to undergo the last test. Some had shaken visibly, while others had tried to cover their trepidation with a show of nonchalance. Bruce had felt only relief. That these hours of waiting could be considered a final test of endurance he never doubted. Suddenly the vast door opened, and the page boy appeared. All ten stood to attention as one body. The bearer began intoning names. Bruce thought his heart would stop, but at last it was his turn: "Reverend Bruce MacAlister."

16

"It's fae Glawgow, richt enough, but its not Bruce's writin'. It's stamped at a different post office, and forby, it's addressed to Mr. and Mrs. MacAlister!"

For once Andrew lost patience with the sleuth of a postman: "Give it to Elspeth, Dugald. The outside has told ye all it will."

Reluctantly Dugald parted with the impressive envelope, and Elspeth slipped the big gully knife under the flap. The three men watching subsided into their chairs. The ritual, observed each time Bruce's weekly missive arrived, would be the same today. Elspeth's expression changed, and a faint smile appeared, almost but not quite smoothing out the worry lines between her brows.

Gran'pa asked the question for the others, "Who is it from, Elspeth, lass? Is the lad right enough?"

"Yes Gran'pa, Bruce is right enough. He's a minister o' the kirk. Oh, Andrew, Gran'pa, he's done it. He's to be ordained!"

"That's never a certificate in such an envelope? Although mind you, it is written on one o' they typewritin' machines!" Dugald had again lifted up the empty envelope to examine it for missed clues, but the other three ignored him.

"The letter is not signed, but it's written by someone who thinks a lot of the boy. Will you read it out to us, Gran'pa? I'll get the tea." Turning as she spoke, Elspeth dabbed her eyes with her apron. Tears of sorrow must be hidden inside, but the joyous kind could be shown without shame.

126

"Dear MacAlister family." With an apologetic smile at Andrew, Gran'pa continued: "I pen these words knowing that the facts I will share may otherwise never have reached you. Your son, Bruce MacAlister, has the makings of a great man. However, I don't believe he will be great, not in the eyes of the world at any rate. More important, he is good. This goodness will set up a response of one kind or another in all those with whom he has contact.

"Although I pray you will never know who writes these words, and I trust Bruce will never be told about or shown this missive, I myself have felt this goodness in a way that showed me up for what I am. The recent 'accident' to his hand brought about some changes in my thinking, but deep down I had always known. I resented his goodness. He is all I wanted to be and can never be. But like you, I can watch him from a distance. I watched from a distance how he managed through terrible pain. A medical friend told me how the tiny broken bones of the hand can cause pain to make the strongest faint, even without movement. Yet your son went on to write every essay and every examination and then stood to give the brawest sermon on Psalm 103 that I have ever heard. By the by, when questioned later on, he told the board of examiners how he got the idea from his 'Gran'pa.' He said his 'Gran'pa' (I quote the word and put it in capitals because that is how your boy said it) taught him to take the words not only of the Gospels and Epistles, but the Psalms as well, and consider them as personal letters from God. This 'Gran'pa' has missed his vocation, I am thinking."

The old man stopped reading to wipe his own streaming face, and Dugald turned away. Clearing his throat, Gran'pa resumed reading:

"I am still not sure why I write all this, except I feel sure, if I did not, he certainly would not. Like Saint Paul, I am compelled. Now, may I ask a favor? May I share, even vicariously—"

"All these big words; have you the dictionary handy Elspeth?"

". . . In the life of this chosen, anointed one? This blythe spirit, who, because of these very qualities, would squirm with embarrassment, in fact would be angered if he knew of this. Use the enclosed draft to pay your way to the ceremony of ordination, and with what is left over make sure he always has a dress kilt in the MacAlister tartan.

"A sincere well-wisher who truly would remain: Anonymous."

"*Anonymous!* He writes letters to the editor of the *Times*, too, a real complainin' body. Always girnin' and greetin' away aboot so many things. I do believe he forgets a' he wrote, because one day he'll be complainin' aboot somethin', and the very next week—"

"Dugald!"

"Aye, mistress?"

"Dugald, you wouldn't be considering coming to Glasgow with us, would you?"

The ensuing silence lasted a full minute by the clock as they waited for Dugald's answer. Suddenly the postie moved, jumping up so quickly that his chair crashed backwards to the floor, bringing Melancholy out of her fireside dream with a frenzied bark of inquiry. Andrew's eyebrows shot up in amazement as he heard the strangled sounds. Elspeth made to rise, but her husband signaled no, while Gran'pa gazed mesmerized at the shaking shoulders under the black serge uniform, so proudly worn by this old family friend. Finally the shaking stopped, and after a hearty blow into his enormous red hanky, Dugald turned from the window to face them.

"I seem to have a bit of a cauld. Och, aye! it's a' this changin' weather!" Gran'pa smiled. Dugald MacPherson's daily excursions with his big bag of royal mail took him many miles in all weathers with never a sniff, but Gran'pa said nothing. Andrew moved toward Dugald, and Elspeth poked up the fire to make a fresh pot of tea.

"Dugald, we would be pleased if ye would come with us to the ceremony in Glasgow! We ken how ye have watched and waited wi' us for just this occasion, and it's only fittin' that ye should share in it. But just go hame and consider it well. There's plenty of time to decide!"

"Aye, Andrew, man, I'll not be needin' to conseeder it. I'll have to get a relief postman and show him the route. Then havin' neither chick nor chiel to bother aboot, it's just my crysants and my auld cat. But never you mind aboot a' that. Alister Og's been dying for the chance to find oot how I grow such bonnie prize-winning crysants onyway. I'll just have to tell him. That's a' there is aboot it. In return he can take care o' Tabby and my hoose." Elspeth gasped. This was sacrifice indeed—the ultimate for Dugald. The rivalry between the two gardeners was known far and wide and had been in progress for longer than she had been in Aribaig.

"Thank you, Mistress Cormack, I'll not have more tea the now, I maun get on wi' my route and start to make my arrangements. I wonder if we'll ever meet Mr. Anonymous?"

Andrew was the first to speak; he waited until Melancholy returned to her corner, after safely escorting Dugald to the bridge. Today, much too abstracted to reach into his sack for the dog's usual tidbit, he merely patted her head before trotting away over the bridge.

"It's a great pity!" Andrew's sigh was deep, and the other two waited for further enlightenment, Elspeth apprehensive, Gran'pa merely curious.

"Aye, this Mr. Anonymous, would you not like to meet him and have a crack wi' him? Especially aboot our laddie, the new Reverend Bruce MacAlister. What conversations we could have! We would find out some of the reasoning behind young Bruce's ideas. Ye ken the ones I'm referring to, Gran'pa?"

"Well, you two might have the time to sit here and have a great philosophical or religious confab, but I have work to do. We have our 'arrangements' to make as well, mind, if we're to be ready in time. Andrew, you know very well that Mr. Anonymous could be anyone. Surely you're not like Dugald in thinking—?"

"Not at all, wife! I know—"

"What I know is that Bruce MacAlister is to be an ordained minister at last, and it didna' come easy for him or us. The professors and kirk rulers who decide these things must know if his 'reasoning,' as you call it, is right or wrong. They must have thought it right enough, or he would not have passed all the exams and such. That's good enough for me and should be for you two as well!" Gathering up the cups from the table, she brushed past the men, and soon they heard the clatter of dishes being washed.

Amazed, the two men stared at each other. Gran'pa Bruce laughingly murmured, "Mother hens and their one wee chick!"

"Mair like a she-tiger and cub the now! Leave her be, Bruce, man. She's mair than pleased, but underneath she is still a bit anxious—trying to make us believe, as she hersel' wants to believe, that our lad is perfect. We know better though! As I was saying about this Mr. Anonymous, what do we know of him? What do we need to know?"

"We know he maun be rich. This bank money order is for a hundred pounds. More than two years' profit for the croft here. There seems to be no way we can send it back to him, as it is, and unless we put it in the fire yonder, we're forced to keep it!"

This time Andrew laughed softly. "We're proud, man, but no' daft. We'll not be puttin' it in the fire. As you say, two years' hard work for us all. We've both got too healthy a respect for siller to throw it away. Aye, he maun be rich enough. What else do we ken aboot him?"

"It's not Mr. Bennett. He would just gie the lad the money, sayin' it was the Lord's biddin', even if that was his way. Bennett has other means o' helpin' Bruce. More spiritual, I'm thinkin'. What a pity he couldna' impart some o' that cheerier way of worship into our boy! I. . . ."

Andrew's face changed. Agreeing as they did on most subjects, this one about worship was usually avoided between them. "We are discussing Mr. Anonymous, I believe, and not the outlandish habits of this Bennett!" His inherent fairness surfaced as he continued, "Maybe we'll just do as Mr. Anonymous suggests. Accept the gifts he sends, not just the money but the confirmation that young Bruce has the right kind of fortitude to be used in his chosen profession. We'll put fifty pounds wi' the rest in his trust fund and continue our plans to go to Glasgow for the ceremony. Only now we can all go. Dugald, too. I've never been there myself, you ken. Bring your maps and books, and we'll go over them again. We can work twice as hard after dinner and make up for the lost time."

Elspeth, busying herself in the scullery, heard and recognized the sounds. Smiling in secret approval, she took her stance at the window. She, too, could make up later for this hour of idleness. Her dream for her lad was near completion. Tucking away the nagging little doubt, she allowed herself to exult in the letter, which now rested securely in her apron pocket. The men could do what they wished with the money, because the written words were what mattered to her. Her heart soared with the dream. What would he be doing at this very minute, her dear one? Her own boy, Reverend Bruce MacAlister. Oh, the sound of that made her whole being rejoice.

She voiced her joy aloud: "Well, my son; I think even your own daddy would have been proud of you this day. And oh, if I could only tell my mother. But nothing will be allowed to spoil this day. I wonder what you are doing the now, Reverend Bruce MacAlister?"

"What shall we do today, my fine fellow? Reverend Bruce MacAlister is it? I suppose you are now too lofty, too high and mighty, to join your more humble classmates in a celebration?" Bruce, ready to agree with Hunter and refuse to join in the so-called celebration, found himself hesitating. What was it Mr. Bennett always said? "If we stay up on our holy pedestal, whatever name we call it, imagining we're so pure, we'll never reach the lost. We must go where they are. 'Be in the world but not of the world.' 'Love the sinner but not the sin.' "

Official results had just been posted on the wall board, and to his true amazement, besides seeing his name on the top of the list of those achieving their divinity degree, another list showed him as first to be recommended for the doctor of divinity. That would mean a further examination and another grilling before the board of examiners. Unsure he wanted to face all that again so soon, Bruce was glad he did not have to decide today. In fact not until he talked to Gran'pa and Andrew, as well as Mr. Bennett, would he make that decision. What his mother would say was a foregone conclusion. Meanwhile the strain of waiting was over; study could be neglected for at least the next few days; and a sense of release swept over him. Even his hand felt better, the tight bandages having been removed yesterday. Recklessly he turned to his tormentors: "Yes! All right, I'll go with you to celebrate. Lead on!"

Bruce peered through the gathering gloom. His eyes seemed to have lost their ability to focus. He knew he must be in the right vicinity, at least these railings round these townhouses looked the same. Finding Mr. Bennett's townhouse, even finding the right crescent, had ever been a challenge. On this terrible night, the night he should have spent praising the Lord for His goodness, the challenge was beyond Bruce. Only a few carriages were abroad in the fog, which seemed to billow round and under him like the waves of the sea. His thoughts also floated in a fog as he wondered what time it could be. Stopping under a gaslight, he peered stupidly at his empty watchchain where it dangled from his fumbling fingers. A sob caught in his throat; Gran'pa's watch was gone! Stumbling and lurching as the pavement rose to meet him, he fell to his knees, clenched fists holding tight to the railings.

"Oh, God! Help me! Bless the Lord, O my soul: and all that is within me. . . ." Then to his everlasting horror, the new reverend, winner of six firsts at the University of Glasgow, including one for rhetoric as well as the recommendation for doctor of divinity, began to cry like a baby.

Thus he might have remained until morning, but his prayer was to be answered in a way far different from any that he or George Bennett would have dreamed or chosen.

"Hello, what have we here? A drunken student by the look of

it! Well, well! Come on, young fellow, let me help you up. If you cannot hold your drink like a man, then you need to be catered to like a woman or a child." The words, spoken in a decidedly English public-school accent, brought Bruce partly out of his stupor.

Pushing back his hat with a shaking hand, where it had slipped sideways across his eyes, Bruce struggled to respond, slurring only slightly, "Do you know where Duke Crescent is, sir? If you can direct me there, I will trouble you no further. I live at number twenty-eight."

"Yes, as a matter of fact I can, because believe it or not, my cabby is waiting patiently to take me to that very address. Are you a protégé of the philanthropist Mr. George Bennett, Esquire, then?"

Bruce, engaged in the futile task of trying to clean off his clothes, looked up in surprise.

"You are acquainted with Mr. Bennett?"

"Indeed I am! That illustrious gentleman has been trying to convert me to his particular brand of Christianity for years, failing of course, but we are still firm friends, and I have been trying to convert him, too." All the time he talked, the stranger was unobtrusively pushing Bruce into the cab. Within minutes they reached the main thoroughfare of Argyle Street, and soon they stopped again. Bruce's mind began to clear, although each word and each jog of the carriage caused a new wave of pain to sweep his body. Still smarting from the remarks about his manliness, he would have died before he would have complained.

Mrs. Oliver opened the door. With only a slight raising of her eyebrows, she led them into the morning room, where George Bennett waited. The friends exchanged glances over Bruce's bowed head before the guest remarked with a laugh, "Found this young fellow-me-lad in the gutter, George, old boy. He seems a bit worse for wear, but I think he'll survive. Maybe you can introduce us?"

"Yes, of course. This is Bruce MacAlister, as of the last few days the Reverend Bruce MacAlister. Bruce, meet my good friend and fellow philanthropist, although he will not admit any good motives, Charles Booth!"

"Reverend is it? Well well! I've found a human one. He needs a 'hair of the dog' as the saying goes, George, my friend. A good stiff brandy would. . . ."

"No! No! No brandy!" Jumping up from the couch, where he had subsided after limply shaking hands with his deliverer, Bruce immediately lost his balance and to his further shame slid to the floor, to lie sprawled helplessly on the carpet in front of the fireplace. George Bennett acted quickly.

"Help me carry him up to his room, Charles, and if you could refrain from further disparaging remarks until we hear his explanation, it would be best."

"Yes, of course. Sorry old chap. Hold on to me, Bruce, my lad. We'll soon have you in your bed, and you can sleep it off. Oh, beg pardon, George!"

Later, the two friends sat in front of the fire, the visitor sipping his brandy, the host stirring thoughtfully at a brimming cup of chocolate. Absently he sprinkled shredded almonds over the thick liquid. This was his favorite nightcap and usually provoked his companion into a kind of mild combat of wit. Tonight however Charles Booth ignored it. His interest and imagination had been stirred, and he wished to discuss the evening's escapade. His curiosity was fully aroused.

"It's a straightforward story, Charles. Tonight's episode is a big surprise to me, but I'm willing to give him the benefit of the doubt. I ask you to bear with me and wait until morning for his explanation. I know it will be the truth."

Laughing again, his guest replied, "All right, George. A protégé of yours, and a new reverend at that, what else but the truth?" The guest stared into the fire for moments before saying, "Now, to get about the business of this proposed royal commission, can I rely on you to be one of my so-called undercover investigators? As you know, that job does not receive payment, and you are one of the few I can trust to speak the truth, even if it is not to the credit of your beloved Christians."

George smiled absently. "My mind being taken up with my, as you say, protégé tonight, Charles, the usual rebuttal of your accusation dies unborn. However, concerning your request about my taking on the job of investigator, you know how I dislike keeping any kind of notes. This promises to require notes of the interminable variety, like the ones you're scribbling now. No doubt you are busy recording your meeting with young Bruce. How you can use it in your statistical campaign I fail to—"

"You wrong me, George. Without your permission I would never do such a thing. Seeing you mentioned this meeting with young Bruce, I suppose you will try to tell me that it is due to some providence of your God that it was I who came upon him in the street yonder and not some press gang or some sharp peeler eager to put him in jail?" George Bennett shuddered visibly. Indeed such had been his thoughts.

"Now it was you who brought up the subject of providence, and to answer your first question, yes, I do believe the Holy Spirit intervened on Bruce's behalf. It would not be the first time, either! You state openly that you think life presents itself as full of chances, and I admit it would seem so. The difference in our findings would appear where I know God is in full control and you think of this as fate, cruel or kind or whatever fancy takes it. Come now, wouldn't it be better if an omnipotent God is in control?"

Charles rose to refill his brandy glass before replying, "I should have known you would snatch any opportunity to preach. Sorry, old chum. Tonight is not the night for my conversion. You might think of this as one of your miracles, but excuse me if I say, a miracle to impress me would be when men stop doing to other men what someone did to your young friend this night. When that happens, it will not be necessary for such as I to step in and pick up boys out of the gutter. In fact, in my kind of miracle, gutters like that would not exist. There would be no dark holes for unsuspecting, gullible fellows to fall into, no need for folks to souse themselves with drink to escape from their awful circumstances. In my kind of miracle, men would consider other men as much as or even more than themselves. . . ." Stopping to catch his breath, Charles was astonished to notice his companion shaking with silent laughter. Offended, he now swore and shouted, "Man, this is no laughing matter, I must protest! Why—"

Immediately contrite, George said, "Forgive me, Charles, but what you have just described is not any human Utopia but is almost word for word how Saint Paul described the Kingdom living, and Jesus says '. . . as you would that men should do to you, do ye also to them likewise.' Paul took up the teaching as he told us to love others '. . . in honour preferring one another.' The Gospels and Epistles are full of such advice."

Only slightly mollified, Charles held up his hand. "All right! All right! I have your meaning, and now, if you have no objections, I am going to retire to the most comfortable room you have so kindly allotted to me. As you reminded me earlier, I have much scribbling to do before I sleep, and I do want to meet this dour Scot under better conditions. Will he be joining us for breakfast?"

"Indeed he will be, and that right early. He has no classes to attend, so he'll not be needing to eat his porridge at six o'clock. Mrs. Oliver will be glad o' that. Shall we say seven o'clock breakfast then? We can have a sleep-in!"

Groaning, but with his good humor fully restored, Charles nodded. "Seven o'clock then, ye old rascal! I'm glad you consider that a sleep-in." Laughing, the friends climbed the stairs together, this time parting on the wide landing.

"Good night, Charles. It's good to have you here!"

"I'm delighted to be here, George. We'll have some more good talk before I have to board the train tomorrow afternoon. Mind you consider what I said about the investigation for the queen's commission."

"Yes, I'll do better than just consider it, I'll pray about it. Sleep well, Charles."

⟨ 18 ⟩

Bruce lay on his back, staring at the ceiling of his room in George Bennett's house. Late moonlight strayed in through the high, undraped window, showing patterns and designs in a black-and-white relief that should have thrilled any artistic soul. Bruce had heard Mr. Bennett speak of these molded etchings, copied from some famous designs of the shapes from nature, such as swans and other creatures, but he, Bruce, considered them ugly. He was failing dismally to distract his mind. He groaned again as his thoughts dragged him backward to the start of it all. He must try to remember about the girl. What had they called her? Biddie! Unable to lie still, now that he was allowing his mind to recall, he rose to walk the floor, his fingers instinctively seeking the watch pocket as he drew on his waistcoat.

"O God! O God! Will I never forget this night? But even as I say that I know I must face it whatever did happen." Peering at the clock on the dresser, he noted the time to be half-past three. Exactly twelve hours since they, his classmates and he, had traversed the quadrangle, on their way to celebrate. *Celebrate?* More like *Saturnalia*. Maybe if he retraced his steps, he would recall if. . . . They had walked to the Ram and Unicorn without any mishaps, and he remembered a foaming tankard being placed in front of him, then another one, both accompanied by smaller glasses of what he knew to be *usquebaugh*, as Gran'pa had called the fiery whiskey, while warning him about its destructive powers.

There his mind balked, showing a blank wall, until the vague memory of being sick in the gutter emerged. Two huge fellows had him by the elbows, and one of them had said, in a threatening way, "Whit'll yer fine professors think o' ye when we tell them how ye took advantage o'oor wee innocent sister Biddie, I wonder?" Unable to respond as another rush of fearful-tasting bile filled his mouth, he had remained mute. Remembering now, he pounded an already-bursting head with his fist. Had he? Searching the haze of memory once more, he recalled someone sitting cosily on his knee. Mercifully his mind went blank, and he slept again.

Awaking later to more gloom-filled thoughts, he began to seek solutions. What a mess life could become! Having escaped the consequences of his own rash actions the time he had hit Colonel Irvine, was he now to suffer doubly for this further folly? In the middle of it all there remained Mr. Bennett's fine gentleman friend. He had not been as grateful as he ought to be to that elegantly dressed dandy. Bruce sighed heavily, dreading the approaching day. What would happen next?

Finally, through his brooding, a few words began to form in his mind. Not the Scriptures, and not even something Gran'pa Bruce or Andrew might have said. Could it have been Mr. Bennett or Fraser Clegg? All unbidden a picture of Professor Alexander's voice came to him: "The most futile word in our language, and I dare to say, any language, is *regret*. Rather, if ye cannot make better of a situation, don't make it worse by harboring regret!" Listening to it the first time, Bruce had thought with lofty disdain, *What a good excuse to get out of wrongdoing.* But the professor had gone on to quote 1 John 1:9.

That's what I'll do now, thought Bruce, *remember I can be forgiven and cleansed and that I have an advocate with the Father.* Striking a Bryant and May from the big box of matches on the table, he lit the lamp beside him and took up his Bible. Of course this is it. . . .

Mrs. Oliver hesitated only seconds outside Bruce's door. Her master had explained briefly about the happenings of the night and told her to wake the lad gently at half-past six, when she called the others. Gently it would be then. Placing the small tray containing the sugared and creamed cup of tea, just the way she knew he liked it, on the table, she removed the Bible from the sleeping fingers and blew out the lamp before she spoke.

"Mr. Bruce! Mr. Bruce! Time to get up. Here's your tea."

The note, tucked under the saucer on his tray, read, "Good morning, Bruce. Be so kind as to join us at half-past seven, in the morning room, for breakfast!" The flourished initials GB hardly seemed necessary, Bruce thought as he splashed his burning face, first with hot and then with cold water from the basin, finishing up with a double splash of cold to catch his breath. Breath! His mouth tasted terrible, and no amount of scrubbing with the willow-stick toothbrush helped. Dabbing quickly at the place where the razor had nicked his chin, he reached for his trousers with the other hand. Funny how his right hand still throbbed so much, reminding him of his other bouts with troubles. Where were his trousers? Oh, the good Mrs. Oliver must have removed them for cleaning. That and the faint odor lingering in his room brought back with a rush the latest memories of the night before and the disastrous "celebration." An embarrassing recollection of his "rescue" from the gutter by that ungodly man, who amazingly enough turned out to be a friend of Mr. Bennett's, flashed through as his thoughts darted hither and thither. Not finding trews, he decided to wear his full highland dress, including his sporran, for the breakfast.

Pride of race and clan, deeply hereditary in Bruce, although never flaunted in his home or in Aribaig, suddenly rose up in the young man as he descended the stairs. The Bruce who sprang from the Munro family ancestry, not to mention the ClanRanald, lifted his head and stiffened his features, his recent shame and distress undergirding the actions. The result, a granite-faced young chieftain, handsome, tall, with blue eyes flashing icy fire, strode into the Bennett morning room, staring straight ahead. To the onlookers he appeared master of the situation as the clock chimed the half hour. Both men, already seated at the table, rose to their feet, and it took George but a minute, his friend slightly longer, to discern the quaking Bruce within the majestic facade: a slight trembling of the chin, a pulse vibrating on the patrician brow, a barely noticeable tremor in the strong, square hand reaching out to shake the visitor's.

Overwhelmed in spite of himself, but quickly recovering his aplomb, Booth said, "MacAlister! MacAlister! Are you related to the MacAlister of Fairlie House, near Aberdeen, I believe?"

"No. 'Tis from the western highlands we are!"

"Sorry!" Booth's eyebrows shot up. *Boorish young upstart! Why if it were not for old George here, I would enjoy bringing it down a peg or two; however for the sake of my friend, I must curb my own predilection for sarcasm and try once more to be civil.*

"So you have finished with the seat of learning, and now you are ready to 'fight the good fight' and revive your flagging church single-handed?" Facing George, whose smile was becoming grim, he pressed on. "The good fight, George, is that not a paradox of terms?"

Risking a glance at Bruce, George decided he would not take the bait Charles was offering. The lad had suffered enough. After praying silently for a word of wisdom, he spoke for the first time since Bruce entered the room, "No! No! Charles. You will not get a rise out of me this morning."

Bruce toyed with the food on his plate; not even the porridge with the thick cream or the crisply curled bacon ringed with eggs smoothly scrambled in butter, placed in front of him now by a concerned and compassionate Mrs. Oliver, could tempt his appetite. Only politeness kept him at the table. He sensed no evil in this stranger, but a stubborn reluctance within himself to admit any good in the other man held Bruce silent. That he was ungodly emanated from the tone in his voice, taking the words he spoke so carelessly, even the very Scriptures, and turning them into mockery.

Suddenly he could stand it no longer. Pushing back his chair, Bruce rose to his full height. "God is not mocked, sir." For a brief span their eyes locked, and the visitor was first to look away. Bowing to his host, Bruce spoke clearly. "Pray excuse me, Mr. Bennett!" Offering no excuse, he waited. George nodded quickly, and Bruce left the room.

"With such a spokesman, God's business is assured wherever your young firebrand spouts his cause, but I must say, George, he seems poorly prepared for the cruel world of indifference awaiting him. I truly hope someone like yourself will help temper that ill-advised zeal before he gets hurt. However, if you have no objections, maybe we could continue our other business. Time is passing as it inevitably does, and . . . well, did you consider my offer?"

"I apologize about young Bruce, but again, Charles, you *did* provoke him. He is much more distressed than your words warrant. Though I wonder. . . .Och, I have no fears for the lad. Surely a few hard knocks await him out there, as you say, and all to temper his mettle. But I'm sure, even as intensely and seriously as he is taking himself and his calling, the Lord will take care of His own. Hm?" Fingering his short beard, George Bennett seemed to go off into a dream for a short space of time. Charles, with surprising patience, waited.

Then, nodding his head as if in reply to a question, George again faced his friend. "Right, then, Charles, you were asking if I considered your request. I indeed prayed about it, and my answer is yes. Now tell me what it is exactly you wish me to do, and how do we begin?"

Mrs. Oliver moved in to clear the table, and the two, deeply engrossed in the welter of papers spread everywhere between plates and dishes, overflowing onto the floor, failed to notice her disapproving clucking. Something more was bothering the housekeeper, and she would have her say.

"Mr. Bennett?" Reluctantly George glanced up.

"What is it, Mrs. Oliver? I asked not to be disturbed this morning."

"Yes, I know, but it is high noon and I—"

"Noon! And I have three others to see in this miserable place before the train departs at five o'clock. George, you know by now what I need. If I leave John Taylor to you, will you explain the matter to him, as he has already agreed? Here is what I want him to do. . . ." In his own zeal the reformer began to go into detail, but Mrs. Oliver would not be put off.

"Mr. Bennett!" Annoyed, he focused on her coolly, without speaking. She continued, "It's young Mr. Bruce!"

"What about him?"

"A dark-skinned person came to the door with a note for him. I could not help but notice the excitement in Mr. Bruce as he read it. Without explaining, he then rushed upstairs to his room and packed his box. I'm afraid he's gone, sir. Here is a note he left for you, and oh, he forgot his trews! I was takin' them up to his room when I found the note and discovered the room cleared of all his belongings! I'm fair worriet, so I am!" With that the stalwart Mrs. Oliver burst into tears. Charles cleared out at once, leaving a disconcerted George to deal with his own domestic problems.

19

Hurrying along Stockwell Street, struggling to keep pace with Bruce, Raju Singh pondered the last few weeks. He and this giant highlander had encountered each other once or twice, and then only briefly in the days before the party, but Raju had heard of him often. Miss Jean's voice, when she spoke the name, told her Indian munshi much more than she dreamed and all he needed to know. The similarity of those thoughts to the ones buzzing through the mind of the man striding ahead of him would have amazed the Indian. Pangs of jealousy had stirred in Bruce's heart at the tone Jean used when she mentioned Raju. That Jean did not consider this man a servant, or even a tutor, could not be hidden.

But Raju was pleased with Bruce. The young man had arrogantly refused Raju's offer to carry the box of books hastily wrapped in the few items of clothing that constituted Bruce's luggage. Why they had to bring the box puzzled Raju not at all. He had learned early in life, first as a child on the mission compound, then later at the army barracks, not to question the sahibs, especially the Scottish sahibs with the kilts. So he followed, running to keep up. Miss Jean had told him what to do in any eventuality so. . . . His thoughts far away, Raju did not notice, until he collided with Bruce, that the giant strides had halted abruptly.

"Why are we almost running, Mr. Raju? The note says one

o'clock under the statue in the square, and it's only a wee bit after ten o'clock." The instinctive reaching for the watch again caused Bruce's heart to sink, but not for long.

The Indian pointed to the clock tower. Was there really one at every crossroads? he wondered. "Twenty past ten, master!"

Bruce looked long and hard at his companion. Was the Indian making fun of him? Oh, well, it mattered little. "Over two hours yet. What should we do in the meantime?"

Raju had wondered that himself, but Miss Jean's orders had been explicit: "Don't arrive at the statue without him!" Maybe she had thought more persuasion might be necessary.

Bruce's brows puckered in the manner his mother and some of his acquaintances would have immediately recognized. She would smile knowingly, while his student friends might have said, "The great Bruce is deep in thought. Watch him!" or some similar remark.

Shyly, Raju touched his sleeve. "Would you come with me to a place nearby? We can wait there safely and have some food. Sahib!"

"What place? Don't call me sahib, and I need no food, Mr. Raju!"

Taking a chance, Raju replied, "Oh, just a place I know, and I won't if you won't. Will you trust me?"

Reaching a decision, Bruce turned to gaze at the man walking beside him, perceiving much more than met the eye. Here stood someone from a far different background, another race, looked upon by Bruce's own kind as inferior, as slaves really meant to serve. Suddenly Bruce saw beyond the visible, far beyond the dirty Glasgow street with its smelly closes and outhouses only half hidden behind the facades of high granite buildings with their ornate clocks and towers. Above his head appeared a break in the clouds, causing the curtain of fog cloaking the city to lift for a moment. A bright, golden ray of sunshine struck the clock face high above them causing a cascading prism of light to envelope Raju. Just as quickly it disappeared, but not before the startled young minister had beheld an almost haloed luminosity bronzing the dark face and turning the hair to bright gold.

Revelation far beyond his understanding made Bruce say, "Lead on, my friend, and don't be daft. Of course I trust you. Let us not be late!"

The place looked and smelled terrible to Bruce, but his new wisdom kept him silent. Last summer, when his ministry had taken him through the tenements, sadly, the back alleys of the Gorbals and the damp, dark cells of the "single ends" had become only too familiar to him. In the last, whole families existed in one room. His experiences then had led him to escape as quickly as possible. Today his companion kept up a running trot, and this time Bruce was the one surprised when they came to a sudden halt.

Raju whispered, "You may be shocked at some of the things you see, but remember those you meet here will be just as surprised at meeting you. I will order food for us, and we will eat as we talk. Try not to be too Anglo-Presbyterian!" At the word Bruce bridled, but after a moment's thought, he found himself smiling guardedly. His sense of humor, flaunted seldom and buried now for months, emerged briefly. He might as well be ready for whatever lay ahead.

In spite of all the warnings and secret signals, the ordinariness of the rooms they entered and even the food came as an anticlimax to Bruce. A veiled woman placed a dish in front of Raju—apparently one plate was to serve both of them— before she disappeared behind the beaded screen. The Indian, wise to the ways of the Anglos, quickly transferred his own helping to a cabbage leaf and passed the plate across the low table to Bruce. No chairs could be seen, so Bruce lowered himself gingerly to the floor, which was covered with a rich Persian rug. Raju produced a fork from somewhere, and Bruce picked it up, discovering he was hungry.

"Excuse me while I pray to thank Jesus!" Blushing, Bruce bent his head. He had almost forgotten to pray. Up to this point, Bruce MacAlister's knowledge of rice consisted of his mother's Sunday-dinner puddings, made with sugar and nutmeg and a few raisins. He liked it well enough, but the rice dish he was eating on this occasion bore no resemblance whatsoever to anything Elspeth ever cooked. Finding small pieces of meat and vegetables mixed in the delicious steaming dish of curry became a game to him, and his plate emptied quickly. Between mouthfuls, he tried to show his appreciation. At home they never said much about the food. It was always good, and to praise one meal more than another might have been interpreted as criticism. Sometimes Andrew would remark that some women improved with age, but as a rule meals were quiet affairs.

Bruce wanted to know about this place and the man who was either host or honored guest—he could not tell which. "Miss Jean often mentioned your name, Raju, but not much more. Where did you come from?" Raju was silent for so long that Bruce glanced up to see if his words had given offense. Recalling a term when they had studied extensively the various cultures and religions of the East and the hundreds of taboos for eating and other activities, Bruce could not be sure. Then remembering Raju for a Christian, he knew such things would have no affect on him.

"Pardon me, Bruce, someday I will tell you where I came from. But now it is better if we start with you. I think you have had many troubles and much pain since Miss Jean's party, and I would hear about them. Is this not so?"

Startled, Bruce looked up again, but the face returning his look was as bland and innocent as a babe's. Bruce knew it was time to tell all. Clearing his throat after swallowing a mouthful from the crystal glass he found mysteriously at his hand, he noted the clear, sharp tang of lemon in the drink before he began to speak. "...So you see, if I did what this Biddie's brothers say I did, maybe I should not even attempt to speak to Jean. But how will I know? I don't believe I could stand the thought of not seeing her, after my hopes have been raised again."

"You will know, and I will help you! As for Jean," they had both discarded the *miss*, "she is aware, as you and I are, that God has destined your paths to be joined. No one, man or woman, shall hinder that. As we came through the other room of this house you no doubt noted some, to you at least, strange people seated about. They are mostly creatures of the night. I am telling them about Jesus in my own way and time, so please do not look so shocked, reverend sir."

Bruce smiled bleakly at this. Who was he to look shocked anymore?

Raju continued, "Anyway these people are my friends. They have ways of finding out things and also of recovering 'lost' property. I have in mind your esteemed grandfather's watch. Ony will retrieve it for you. About the money. We will pay it to keep the brothers of Biddy quiet. A small price to pay for a good lesson. Now come and meet my friends. No, do not pull back your righteous skirts, like the Pharisee. Oh, I beg pardon, Scotti sahib, I did not mean to make a joke."

Bruce leaped to his feet, adjusting the pleats of his kilt as Raju spoke. For a minute he could not look at the Indian. Then suddenly the incongruity of the whole matter dawned on him, and he grinned shamefacedly as he flushed crimson.

"Some of these are your countrymen, some mine. Just remember Christ died for each one and would mingle with their like. We can do no less than our Master." Briefly Bruce felt his hackles rise again as the dark-skinned fellow presumed to teach him his business. Then he remembered: His own awkward situation put him at a great disadvantage. With his beloved waiting, as he waited, for the hours to pass, they were both deeply obligated to this strange man, servant, friend, advisor, who could plumb these depths.

"Let it be so for now!" he found himself muttering, and if his strange companion heard, he made no answer.

148

$-\cdot\circ\cdot\lessgtr\{$ **20** $\}\gtrless\cdot\circ\cdot-$

"**Y**ou don't know what you're saying, Jean. For one thing your father would kill me, and for another I've no money and no parish yet. And wouldn't Mrs. MacIntyre be upset and. . . . What about my mother and Gran'pa?"

"That's why I'm suggesting eloping! There are so many people involved who'll make objections, and even if they all agreed, it would be a year or more before we could be alone together. I thought and prayed so hard about it. Then suddenly my mind cleared, and everything fell away except that we love each other so. It's just you and me, Bruce, and it's our lives. Why should all those others, much as we care for them, be allowed to keep us apart . . .?"

"It's speechless I am! I don't know what—"

"Don't say anything else, then. We *do* love each other, don't we? After all, it's me, the bride, who has the most to sacrifice. A white satin wedding dress and a reception with a cake and all the frills, and yes, I would like these things, but they add up to nothing compared to just being your wife. If you want me, that is!"

"If I want you? I've thought of nothing else for weeks. Supposing I agreed—which I haven't yet—what would we live on? My degree is still wet with the university ink! My family is preparing even now for the going-out ceremonies next week. Oh, no! It's just *not* possible!" At that Jean began to cry, but hiccuping between sobs, she had more to say.

"Reverend Bruce MacAlister, if I didn't know better, I'd say Daddy was right, and you *are* a coward. To say nothing of shaming a girl in front of our best friends! Knowing you're not, I'll try to answer your objections. By the time your parents arrive, we'll be man and wife. For money! I have fifty pounds, which I will lend you for a few hours, until what's mine is yours. We will tell no one else until it is too late to change it."

Suddenly Bruce's face cleared, and he began to laugh. For a moment Jean looked offended, and then she joined in. His eyes were on the statue of Sir Walter, high above them, as he recalled the day they first met.

"Let me tell you something that may just change your mind, my bonnie schemin' lassie. Ten of your fifty pounds might have to go to paying off a girl called Biddie. She and I spent some time together last night, when your reverend here set about celebratin' with all the other great students. We were in a pub. Then there is the small matter of your father's injury, and if that's not enough, I'm afraid I've offended my good host Mr. Bennett, and oh, what am I saying? It's not to be thought of."

"If you are expecting me to have the vapors about this Biddie, I'm sorry to disappoint you. Don't forget I lived half my life in India. . . . Bruce, listen to me and allow yourself to think. I've prayed about this, and I am very sure. I could not say all these things otherwise. If you are not sure, then I'm sorry I've made a mistake, and there's no more to be said, except to repeat it's our lives. Why waste our time on folderols that matter not a whit?" They sat in silence for what seemed a long time. Out of hearing but within sight, on another bench, Raju and a stiffly disapproving Betsy waited. Half an hour had elapsed since Bruce and Raju entered the square, and without words or preamble, Betsy had risen to give him her place and walked to the other seat, followed by Raju.

Bruce turned to look at them and then back to Jean. "We're all mad!" he muttered, but he moved closer to this daring girl who had his heart and shyly grasped her hand. "You're not giving me an ultimatum, are you, Jean?"

"Not exactly. I still think we are meant for each other, but here is the alternative. If we wait, it will be years—maybe never. Daddy will not allow your name to be mentioned, and Mummy is saying we are going to America as soon as Daddy's next term is finished. They are determined not to leave me with Granny again and—"

"You have shown me a part of your nature I never suspected. When you make up your mind, you don't dillydally, do you? The last time I heard your voice, you were screaming how I had killed your father."

"I'm sorry about that, but Granny explained to Mr. Bennett and—

"I am the sorry one. Who else knows about this, forby these two?"

"Only Peter. I had to tell him so he could get the license for us." She opened her handbag as she spoke and removed a flimsy piece of paper, faintly resembling a five-pound note, and handed it to Bruce. He sat gazing at it, unaware of the passing of time. Feeling her small hand slip back into his, he made his decision. She was right. What did they have to lose? Once married, they would all just have to accept it, even Mam and Gran'pa. Somehow he felt sure Andrew would understand.

"You win, Miss Jean Irvine. I accept your proposition. I should have known, that day you tried to meet me beneath Sir Walter, you were a brazen hussy and that you were in reality settin' your own cap at me!"

The other players in this real-life drama knew their parts well, intensifying Bruce's feeling of having entered a theater where he was only one of the actors in a play. Under mild protest, he had attended a theater with Peter once, and these actions seemed similar. Three of the supporting cast came from offstage and took control, while he unerringly obeyed without having to think further.

"Be anxious for nothing!" Jean's admonition after his last feeble protest still rang in his ears when he stood before the aged cleric, listening to the tired voice intone the incredible words that would link him for life to this girl he hardly knew. Peter had told him the old fellow had already married six couples that day, most of them rushed for different reasons than theirs, and it was only four o'clock in the afternoon.

Too quickly it was over, and Peter was grasping his hand to shake it exuberantly, as Peter did everything. Betsy, who had stood rigid and disapproving, obviously here under coercion, broke down and started to sob. Jean, flushed but still calm, hugged the maid to soothe her.

"It's all right, Betsy, everything is all right. Granny will not blame you, and once I explain, she, too, will understand we had to do it this way. Now we must all take our Lord's advice. Not only does He tell us to be anxious for nothing, He inspired Paul to say in everything give thanks and to say rejoice. Now Peter, you have Paddy McShane's brougham waiting to take us to Fergusons for high tea, and I gave Cook the letter, with strict instructions to give it to Granny only if we weren't back in time for tea at Strathcona. Raju—"

"Could you stop talking for just a minute, Mrs. MacAlister?"

All eyes turned to the speaker in amazement. A stunned silence followed Bruce's words. Jean, who up until that moment had been the activator of this whole conspiracy—for what else could it be called?—visibly wilted. The striving drained away, leaving a radiant young woman who had achieved her heart's desire. With a gasp she moved toward Bruce, but he was quicker. One stride brought him to her side, and he gathered her up in his arms. To Peter he called out, "Lead on, MacDuff! To the magical chariot and the wedding feast you've no doubt planned. After that you can all make your exit, because I'll have plans of my own!"

The small party had reached the pavement, where a grinning Raju held the carriage door open. Paddy, seated regally on top, had contributed to the occasion by wearing his top hat and swallow-tailed coat. So dressed, he represented the only formal dress of the day, although Bruce still wore his kilt. Stripped of fanfare or formality, the proceedings still exuded a natural dignity of a kind that could not be bought. Peter's reply to the bridegroom's remarks died unspoken. The return train tickets to Oban, his planned wedding gift, remained in his pocket. That highlander had things well under control. Raju, the silent watcher, kept his thoughts hidden. If they included awed amazement at the shift in the Scottish sahib's fortunes in such a short space of time, only he knew, and most important, his Jean was happy!

"You're very quiet, Andrew, and I know you're not anxious about the farm. So something else is bothering you." Elspeth glanced round the railway compartment. Dugald and Gran'pa Bruce appeared to be peacefully sleeping.

"No, I'm not anxious, wife, just curious. Don't forget, I've never been this far south afore, and the land is changin' every time I blink my eyes. Where are we the now, Gran'pa?" Before the older man could reply, Dugald, the self-appointed tour guide, forestalled him.

"We just passed a place called Arrochor, an' it's only two or three miles fae Loch Lomond. That hill ower there is the ben!" Every eye followed the postie's pointing finger, to drink in the pastoral scene. Gran'pa Bruce rubbed his eyes. He had no objection to Dugald's becoming guide. In fact his own mind was busy with other matters. He had not been asleep when Elspeth asked Andrew if he was anxious, and Andrew might not be, but he, Bruce, discerned some anxiety coming from Elspeth herself. Since the time when their plans had been confirmed and the train time settled, she had sat down to write to her son, taking immense pride in addressing the envelope *Reverend Bruce MacAlister*. That was almost two weeks ago now. Although a letter had been delivered by special messenger, from Mr. George Bennett, saying he himself had to go to London, but his home would be at their disposal for the duration of their visit to Glasgow, they still had no letter from the lad, just the telegram. In the four years Bruce had been away in Glasgow, he had never gone a week without sending a letter, but it was now three weeks since the official document informing them of the passing-out ceremonies had arrived. That fact, and the telegram, were what caused that puzzled frown to crease Elspeth's brow. The strangeness of the wording in the telegram had done nothing to ease her confusion. Watching her from time to time, through hooded lids, the older man was unheeding of the scenery flashing by. In his head the train wheels beat out the words of the telegram, ordinary enough words but so unlike Bruce: *Meeting your train. Central Station. Bruce.*

Snatching an opportune moment to speak briefly to Elspeth, whose agitation grew noticeably worse the nearer they got to Glasgow, he said: "He'll be awright, Elspeth, lass. The auld saying 'No news is good news' has a lot o' truth in it, ye know."

"I know, Gran'pa. It's just that it's so unlike him. Oh, how I wish I could get rid of this feeling."

"Well, you know my advice aboot courtin' trouble, an' the Lord Himsel' says, 'Sufficient unto the day is the evil thereof.' I take that to mean it's bad enough to concern ourselves when we know somethin's amiss, but don't go lookin' for troubles."

Elspeth looked closely at the old man, who had been so staunch a help to her and Bruce through the years. She smiled. "Yes, Gran'pa, you're right as always. We'll enjoy it while we may."

Jean stood about ten paces behind Bruce, her eyes following his agitated pacing, back and forth, back and forth, as they awaited the train from Fort William.

Bruce's jollity, displayed since the elopement, had dissipated. A strong desire to run for it almost overwhelmed him. Watching the railway porter set up the barricade separating the arrivals from the departures made him swallow convulsively. The train would be here in less than two minutes. Suddenly he squared his shoulders. He was done with running away. There would be some awkward moments to face, but face them he must. It was not as if he were sorry for marrying Jean. Far from it. Yet looking back, he wondered how it could all have gone so smoothly and easily. They had prayed as soon as they found themselves alone together, and everything seemed so right. Within the bliss of their short honeymoon he pushed thoughts of his mother aside. Not even the thought that she would soon be here for the ceremony bothered him. But now the moment was upon him. Jean was out of his sight, behind him, where he had told her to stand. These next few minutes were his alone.

With a great roaring and gushing of steam, the giant engine screeched to a standstill, with carriages and compartments telescoping behind it. Doors sprung open, and the train poured forth its human cargo.

Jean recognized them at once. No mistaking the look of Bruce's mother, with her high, proud brow and the finery of two decades ago gracing her slight form. The three men behind Elspeth, without speaking a word, nevertheless conveyed volumes to the quaking young bride. During this past week, Jean had begged and pleaded with her husband to write a letter to Aribaig, but he would not.

"No, all my life I've been avoiding facing up to my own predicaments. I will confront the matter like a man." The confrontation was upon them. Sensing eyes on her, Jean half turned to find one of the older men gazing at her. His look was mildly benevolent and reassuring. This must be Gran'pa Bruce. Kindness exuded from him, and he completely fulfilled his grandson's description. In a tweed hunting cap and jacket, he was every inch the gamekeeper so popularized by the press as depicting Queen Victoria's Scottish servants. Giving herself a shake, as she recognized her thoughts to be deliberate sidetracks away from happenings taking place on the station platform, instinctively Jean moved closer to her husband. Then she saw Elspeth's stricken face. No other word could describe it. Stopped in her tracks, Jean found her arm being clasped by the tweed-clad figure of Gran'pa.

"Pardon me, but would you be Miss Jean Irvine by any chance?"

With a nervous little laugh she answered, "No, sir, I am not Miss Jean Irvine anymore. I'm Mrs. Bruce MacAlister, and you must be Gran'pa Bruce. I'm very pleased to meet you!"

Unable for the moment to truthfully say he, too, was pleased to make her acquaintance, the senior Bruce clutched the diminutive hand outstretched to him. His first and entirely irrelevant thought was *This hand feels how a woman's hand should feel, soft and firm.* Then his mind swiveled to Elspeth's and some other womens' hands. Elspeth's hands, though small, were workworn and rough. His own mother's hands floated before him. Large, square, capable hands. Then Morag of the bonnie face, his wife, dead these many years; her hands had been small, too, but had had that plebian appearance and. . . .

"Could I have my hand back, please?" Dropping it as if it were a red-hot coal, he floundered like any callow youth speaking to a lass for the first time. Struggling for words, he was saved from speech as Dugald stepped to his side.

Bruce gripped his mother's arm firmly. For a minute there, when he had broken the news, he had thought she might fall, but she had rallied. Then her face seemed to shrink as it registered shocked amazement, disbelief, and horror. Her carefully built basket of dreams crumbled. But almost at once Elspeth's inherent fortitude surfaced. The station platform tilted back to its normal plane and clattered around the small group. A porter bustled up importantly and whispered to Bruce in a loud aside, "If you will follow me, Mr. Bennett's carriage awaits you."

Still in a daze, Elspeth allowed herself to be led to the waiting conveyance, closely followed by a slightly bewildered group of men, listening to, had they but known it, a completely out-of-character Jean as she chattered on about the historical significance of their surroundings.

"Oh, I think I shall hear the inane echo of my own voice, for all the world like that guide in the zoo, forever. What will they think of me? Your mother, so dignified, strangely resembling that portrait of Queen Victoria in Granny's library, and your stepfather—I do believe he was secretly amused. Oh, Bruce, your Gran'pa, he is all you ever promised and more. As for Dugald, words cannot describe him. I—"

"Whoa, Jean, whoa, you're off again. This time it's *my* ears that are ringing with your many words. But it's all right, the worst of it is over." Bruce would never forget the expression on his mother's face, but the worst was indeed over. The small party, planned by Beulah to welcome his family, could only be an anticlimax now, and as for the ceremonies at the university, why they would be easy in comparison to the day just past.

"So, it's Reverend and Mrs. Bruce MacAlister. Well, well, I must say I'm not surprised, not a bit surprised." The speaker, Dr. Peter Blair, Senior, truly had forgotten an earlier episode, when he had witnessed evidence rather than formed suspicions of a romance between the couple. "Congratulations, I must drink a toast to the bride and to your future. My advice, fill your hoose wi' bairns, an' ye'll not have to look elsewhere for your joys. You'll not have your sorrows to seek either, but the joys will far outweigh them. Where's my tardy son wi' that Glenlivet. A proper toast, eh, Peter, my boy? Will ye join me in it? He's a doctor now, you know, even if he's not coming into my practice. Goin' in for this highfalutin social reform, but och weel, he'll be back. We'll drink to that, too, eh, son?" None among his listeners remarked upon Dr. Blair's toast, but only Peter joined him. The party, different in so many ways from that earlier, almost-tragic one in the spring, was going well enough, considering the circumstances.

Then the hostess, wearing a "cat who licked the cream" smile and easily the happiest among those affected by Bruce and Jean's marriage, surprised her guests by responding to Dr. Blair: "Yes, doctor, although I do not condone the use of alcoholic beverages, I believe the concept of a toast has merits as a means of extending a blessing, one upon another, if one does not have the benefit of a strong faith in God."

"Begging your pardon, Mistress MacIntyre, but this toast is my idea, and I will propose it. A toast then to reform, social or otherwise. Any kind of reform that promises to change the miserable human condition for the better—no, that more than promises, vows, and swears to improve their condition. It seems to me the reason we gather here to celebrate is, in reality, to honor all those among us who have spent the best years of their youth, as I did mine in my day, preparing for bringing that reform about. . . .So—"

"You were to give a toast, Father, not a lecture or a platform speech for—"

"The cheek of it! Just because you have a certificate to practice medicine does not give you the right to speak to your parent like that."

"Now, Father, don't get upset. Every dog has his day, and this is mine. All my life I've had to listen to you and your speeches. Now it's my turn. I will not put on a veneer of humility, because I've earned this day, and I'm going to enjoy it. A toast, eh? All right. To all those reformers present: those with a parchment to prove it and those without, those who will do it on the human level and those who aspire to a higher level. Here's to us!"

"Hear, hear," and, "Cheers!" greeted Peter's oration, and those who still lingered, now that the main body of guests had left, began to drift round the room. The homemade wine used to drink the toast was very mild, but evidently young Peter had indulged in his father's Glenlivet. One of the voices responding to his toast caught Peter's attention. This was not a Glasgow voice, nor was it even Scottish, but he liked the sound of it just the same. He set about finding the owner.

21

Peter's mind sobered quickly as he turned to concentrate on what Faye Felicity was saying.

"Agatha, this is Dr. Peter Blair. Dr. Blair, my niece, Agatha Rose Gordon, transplanted from the Yorkshire dales." Not recognizing himself immediately, Peter turned, but Dr. Blair, Senior, had disappeared again.

"Sorry, Miss Gordon, but it's not every day a man becomes a doctor and then meets a living Yorkshire rose. It would seem too much good fortune for anyone."

"Excuse me, Aunt Beulah needs me. I'll leave you two to discuss reform or roses or whatever you like. Just don't leave the party until I come back, Aggie." Faye Felicity moved away as she spoke.

"I love that name, Aggie. May I call you Aggie?"

"Yes, Dr. Blair, if you like, but my middle name is Rose and. . . ." But Peter laughed tipsily.

"Not Dr. Blair. Please, call me Peter. Tell me, where have they been hiding you all my life? Oh, I remember, the Yorkshire dales. It's a crime, that's what it is. What do you do there?" Agatha smiled, but before she could reply, Peter continued, "I expect the terrain is not much different from the hills of Fife or the plains of Brittany for that matter. I've been to many places on my walking tours, but I'm ashamed to admit I've not been to England. Let's find a place to sit, and you can tell me about

Yorkshire." Aware that he was babbling, Peter put his hand on the girl's elbow and led her rather unsteadily across the room to a secluded corner.

"Yes, doctor, I mean Peter, I will tell you about Yorkshire, if you like." She hesitated, and the besotted Peter, leaning close to catch every phrase and nuance of the soft, sweet voice, smiled in what he thought to be an encouraging fashion. "But I can also tell you a bit about London. Auntie Faye and I spent a term with the London Missionary Society, and I could give you a firsthand description of the desperate need for that reform you spoke about. I could not help overhearing your, er, toast . . . and . . . ."

An hour later Bruce found the two still sitting in the corner, completely engrossed in each other. He whispered to Jean, "Who is that with our new physician? She seems to have monopolized him for the whole evening!"

"She's Faye Felicity's niece, I thought you had been introduced earlier. As for monopolizing, I think your dear Doctor Peter had something to do with that. Why when we arrived he was sharing his view with anyone who would listen, and it appears he has found a willing audience."

Agatha Rose gazed, enthralled, at Peter. A beaming Peter, just as enthralled, had become the willing slave of this blossoming rose.

Meanwhile, in another corner of the vast drawing room, some other important confrontations were taking place.

"It's most civil of you, I'm sure, Mistress MacIntyre, to entertain us in this manner, and I thank you on behalf of my family."

"No thanks are necessary, Mr. MacAlister. Since my granddaughter is now a member of the same family, does that not make us related in some way?"

"To be sure, mistress, but under the circumstances I would have thought—"

"Shame on you, sir, of what circumstances do you speak? If those two were not intended for each other by the Almighty

Himself, then my name is not Beulah MacIntyre." Blue eyes twinkling under raised brows, the senior MacAlister did not quite dare to wonder aloud how much help the Almighty had received from the same Beulah MacIntyre. That lady continued to speak, and the extremely perceptive highlander recognized her deep need to justify her recent actions.

"Mrs. Cormack is rather less enthusiastic about the union of our families, I fear; but then the mother of the bridegroom is traditionally reluctant to part with a son, is that not so?" Politely ignoring the question, he attempted to defend Elspeth.

"You must forgive Elspeth. She has suffered much and had high expectations for the lad. More than she should have, mayhaps, and I ken it will take her longer than you and me to realize just how indeed this turn of events is the Lord's will and plan for the young ones."

"I understand some of what you say, Mr. MacAlister, but I fail to see how being married to my Jean can be anything but beneficial to this mother's hopes and plans. Why Jean has—"

"Say no more, mistress. I have seen and heard enough to form my own opinion of your Jean, and it closely resembles your own. Just give Elspeth time. She'll come round in her own way, and when that happens, we'll all know about it. For the now we should all take Gamaliel's advice, which seems to me meant mainly allowing the Holy Spirit to work through all of us, in case we find ourselves working against God."

"I see you are a man of wisdom. Since my dear husband, the Reverend Dr. MacIntyre—you may have heard of him—went into the presence of the Lord, I have not heard the Holy Scriptures spoken of in quite the same way—as if we could apply them to daily life. Mind you, George Bennett has some leanings in that direction, but he tends to go to extremes. I perceive you to have both feet firmly planted on the ground even as you reverence God."

"Thank ye, mistress, you are too generous with your compliments. Looking deeper into it, you might see how I see, possibly how Dr. Gamaliel saw, an easier way to solve any dilemma."

"Say what you please, it still denotes wisdom in the situation. Very well, I will not push attention on Mrs. Cormack but will await her coming to me. Now, before I resume my sadly neglected duties as hostess, I would hear some more of your practical expository of God's Word. You will pardon an old lady for her memories I'm sure."

Leaning toward Beulah, to gallantly deny her description of herself, Bruce suddenly laughed merrily. She was an old lady, and he was an old man, but they could share these moments in time now. The older ones knew life need not be so grim.

Elspeth, seated with Andrew a short distance away, could not hide her disapproval. Speaking in a cold, tight voice, another legacy of Hugh Munro, the advocate, she addressed Andrew. "The old man has been smitten, too, with the wiles of these city women. Young and old they seem to mesmerize the MacAlister men. Look, Andrew, some folk are starting to leave. Can we not go now? The hostess seems to have forgotten her manners."

Andrew spoke firmly, "Wife, you are not being fair. You forget you were once a city woman yoursel', and who knows how many of the people of Aribaig said that about you at first? Elspeth, I've tried to be patient with ye in this time of change, but now I must insist you be more civil. Not only to us of your family, but to our son's wife and her grandmother!" Andrew's words fell on stony ground; his wife refused to be appeased. Had she not been so deeply embedded in her grief, she would have remarked on his use of terms like *insist* and *demand* or anything that could be classed as critical of her. As it was, she took immediate offense and resumed the stony silence and rigidity of manner that spoke more eloquently than any words.

Sighing and resigning himself to the fact that today would not yet bring about the reconciliation he so fervently longed for, Andrew prayed silently for patience and the right words. Wisely refraining from speaking further as the thought

Discretion is the better part of valor flowed through his mind, he smiled. A phrase like that had to be the Lord's answer to the prayer, because he, Andrew Cormack, had never used the saying before. Glancing round the elegant room, emptying rapidly, he decided it was time for them also to leave.

The reception was indeed winding down. Invitations, so carefully calligraphed by Faye Felicity and Agatha, then proudly delivered by Paddy McShane, had read thus: "Mrs. Beulah MacIntyre, in the absence of her daughter and son-in-law, Colonel and Mrs. Cameron Irvine, and on their behalf, cordially invites you to a reception chiefly to honor her granddaughter, Jean Mary Beulah, on the occasion of her recent marriage to the Reverend Bruce John MacAlister of Aribaig, Invernesshire. . . . As it is our custom, at this season of the year, to honor those of our student boarders who have gained their degree in whatever field of endeavor, the second, but by no means secondary, purpose for this reception is to honor, along with Reverend MacAlister, Dr. Peter Thomson Blair, of Burntisland, Fifeshire. RSVP." There followed the dates, times and place of the affair, and. . . . "P.S. Also in accordance with our tradition, the graduating men will be expected to entertain the gathering with a speech."

Unlike Peter's oration, Bruce's had been short and formal. In face of his mother's stolid refusal to speak to him and her tangible disapproval, he merely thanked his hostess and her guests for the honor of their presence and their gifts.

In the back regions of the George Street house, another party was in progress. Paddy McShane was one of the speech makers, but Bennie was not being outdone. Mrs. Oliver, whose culinary additions to the feast had been considerable, was seated comfortably in Cook's own armchair. Betsy had brought in a footstool from the parlor for the visitor's feet. A mild argument had arisen between Paddy and Benny, and Mrs. Oliver thought the time ripe for her to intervene.

"You know, you are both right to a certain extent, but

Benny, you are being a wee bit hard on the young reverend. Certainly his speech sounded stiff and strained. That's not to be wondered at with his mother glowering daggers through him and Miss Jean, since they arrived here, but I'm agreein' wi' Paddy, too. A short stiff speech doesna' make Master Bruce a Pharisee. Far from it. In my opinion he is one of the Lord's anointed and will rise up through hard times to do great exploits for God."

Benny turned on her fiercely. "And what are you, Mrs. Oliver, to say the likes o' that? A fortune-teller, maybe? We should plead the blood o' Jesus ower us to hear such things. It's this hoose and the devil drink I've seen bein' consumed by some of the guests. Idolatry is what it should be called . . . . I—"

"Now, now, Benny, my lad, none o' your name callin', or somebody might say ye're tarred wi' the Pharisee yersel'." This time it was Cook who spoke.

"Idolatry indeed. Not in this place." Paddy had risen to advance threateningly, but Cook stopped him with a wave.

"We'll hae none o' that in my kitchen, if you please. Be seated, gentlemen. I'm agreein' wi' my friend Norah here. I've always noticed something different aboot young Mr. MacAlister mysel', but I can understaun his mother's feelin's, too. After all, she doesna ken Miss Jean like us. Norah, I believe, too, the Good Lord has great things for the minister, an' if that's so, all the sayin's an' doin's of his friends—or his enemies—will make no difference."

Betsy had a word to say here, "As for bad-mouthin' Dr. Peter, it's only high spirits and the wrong kind of teachin' from his faither that makes him drink so much elderberry at parties. . . ."

Even Paddy gave a snort of derision at this naïveté. "Are ye a we'an then, Betsy? Why, when I brung the two doctors this nicht, we made not one, but two, stops at a pub. At first I thought they were meanin' a place in Fife, but now I know they spoke o' the bottles o' whiskey when they said 'Glenlivet.' " The women laughed uncertainly at this, but Benny remained impassive and scowling.

Paddy had more to say, but wisely he changed the subject. "Aye, speakin' o' places and wearyin' for hame. Although I have drove my jauntin' caur for forty years in Glesga, I still have whiles when I weary for Donegal. Even the day, as ye spoke of the second sight, I am minded o' a woman in my village who had it. For a farthin' she would tell you everything aboot yer future, and sometimes she would just look at ye an' get awful quietlike, puttin' the fear o'—"

Benny jumped to his feet. "Please, Mr. McShane, I maun rebuke yer words in the name of Jesus. What I said about Reverend MacAlister and what you have just told us are as different as night from day. I believe I had the word of knowledge, but I see it was out of place for me to speak of it here. I'll say no more until I have spoken to Mr. Bennett, upon his return."

Silence fell on the group for a few moments until the sound of a bell jangled into the stillness. Mrs. Oliver said, "There's the signal for us to leave. Betsy, you must bring Mrs. Wilson to visit me soon. I have visitors on Tuesdays and Saturdays at three o'clock. . . ."

"Who else but Dr. Blair would leave an empty wineglass on top of the piano like that?" Faye Felicity sounded bitter as she sniffed at the offending glass. "Just as I thought, no homemade elderberry ever gave that kind of peatty aroma."

Absently Beulah answered, "It's not like you to be unkind, Faye Felicity. I recall the last occasion when Dr. Blair attended a soiree; you were loud in his camp with some high-sounding reasons to excuse his 'weakness' as you called it then."

"Was I? Oh, well, that just proves how wrong those theories can be. It may be too late for the senior Blair, but that's no excuse for the younger one. I wonder if it's a case of 'like father, like son'?"

Ah-ha! So thats it! thought Beulah, and her eyes grew soft as they lingered on her goddaughter. "Where is Agatha Rose?" Beulah's customary use of two names included the young niece, and she glanced round the empty room as she spoke.

"The last I saw of her, she was marching down the garden path, a drunken doctor on each arm!"

"Faye Felicity!" This time Beulah's indulgence toward the other woman's gross breach of manners disappeared in shocked amazement. Never before had she heard Faye Felicity speak so harshly. At that moment the French doors opened, and a flushed and slightly disheveled Agatha Rose stepped through.

"Sorry, Auntie. I . . . ," she got no further.

"Where have you been? Don't you know I'm responsible to your father for you? Your conduct tonight has been disgraceful and—"

Beulah stepped between the two younger women. "Stop this at once! This is my home, and I apply the rules and accept the responsibilities. Agatha Rose, I believe you do owe us an explanation."

"Yes, as I began to say, I merely stepped out to the summerhouse with Dr. Blair. We were discussing social reform, and you know how interested I am and—"

"Hah! That may have been your reason to begin with, but—" Again Beulah took a hand: "Faye Felicity, allow me to handle this. Agatha Rose, your aunt is right. Young girls should not go out with young gentlemen of such short acquaintance, unchaperoned."

"Auntie Faye told me herself that you entertained the more-enlightened views of behavior but I wonder if she even does. I am nearly twenty years old, one year younger than Jean, but even so I am shocked at your lack of trust. I am sorry, but—oh, please excuse me. . . ." With that, Agatha Rose ran out of the room. The other two sat on in stunned silence after the door slammed.

Finally Beulah spoke, "I must say I'm rather surprised, myself, at your reactions, Faye Felicity. What has come over you?" Faye's laugh, strained and unreal, on the brink of hysteria, answered the question. Then she gave in.

"We both know, Auntie Mac. It's the age-old elder-brother syndrome, as Freud would say, did he quote the Bible. Slightly out of context, but here I sit yelling, 'I've been here all the time, serving you faithfully, doing what is right, never stepping out of line or behaving unseemly. The Far Country never called me, or if it did even faintly, I chose to ignore it.' Oh, Auntie Mac, what shall I do? It's not fair." The last word ended in a wail, and Beulah, sighing faintly, subsided into her chair and held out her arms. Jean's footstool had disappeared somewhere, but the large brocade cushion would serve the same purpose.

Stroking the shining dark head, she whispered, "You quote the Master's parable well, up to a point, but you are missing the next part. Listen: 'Son (or daughter, of course) thou art ever with me, and all that I have is thine.' He goes on to say they must rejoice for the lost one who is now found. To bring it up to date for us now, may I remind you Jesus does not promise an easy road. He never mentions fairness as we think of it in human terms. In fact the opposite is true most of the time. Granted, some of His chosen—and never doubt you and I are included in that number—may have their way smoother than others. That is not nearly as important as we think. Allow all this to leave your mind now as you remember the Psalmist's request, 'Make thy way straight before my face.' Accept that with no question as you 'lean not on your own understanding. . . ,' which may be too sharp for your own good, Faye Felicity, 'but in all your ways acknowledge Him, and He shall direct your paths." Faye had ceased crying, and now as the clock in the hall boomed the single hour, both women moved to their knees.

In the room upstairs, which she shared with her aunt, a subdued Agatha Rose waited. The young girl, too, prayed: "Dear Lord Jesus, help Auntie Faye and Great-aunt Mac to understand I did nothing wrong, but help me, too, to tell them that Peter and I are meant for each other every bit as much as Jean and Bruce. Now Lord Jesus as I lay me down to sleep. . . ."

Faye Felicity smiled as she slipped into the big bed beside Aggie's slight form. The sweet innocent. The Lord would help her to endure without murmuring, even to the point of aiding this romance, if such it turned out to be.

As for the young MacAlisters, the moment the last guest had departed, they had disappeared to the rooms prepared for them. *That* romance seemed to be set fair for a "happy ever after" life of smooth sailing.

Faye Felicity sighed deeply once more. Her thoughts just before sleep turning, strangely enough, not to the new doctor or minister, but to a certain dark-skinned man, closely knit with this family, yet so far from her as the North Pole from the South.

22

"**D**id the mistress get a letter from Miss Jean the day, Betsy?"

"Och, Cook, I would've told you if she had. No, it's aboot two weeks since she got a letter, but mind you, she had one every week for a while afore that. Away up there on that island, it's a wonder they have ony post at all." Betsy vigorously beat the eggs for the pudding Cook would make soon, and froth rose high in the bowl as the maid put all her "elbow grease" into the task.

"Easy on the eggs, Betsy, lass. You don't need to beat the daylights oot o' them, ye ken."

"I'm sorry, Cook. I just get boiling mad when I think o' Miss Jean away in thon wilds withoot ony help in the hoose, an her expectin' an'—"

"Betsy, you should've went wi' them when ye had the chance. Then we should ken she had somebody of her ain to look after her. Maybe, when the bairn comes, the mistress'll gie ye another chance to go."

"Och! Ye ken fine that, fond as I am o' Miss Jean, I'm feared to go to thon wild country. The mistress showed us that map one day, and then the picture card Miss Jean posted to me! The waves so high on thon black, raggedy rocks, wi' no sandy beaches like there is at Saltcoats. Oh, no, I hope she doesna' ask me again. . . ." The maid's real anxiety showed on her homely face, and the ready tears began to flow.

"Aye, well, we've enough to do the day wi' that Miss Gordon and her niece back to stay and the dinner party the night. Who else is comin'? There's Mr. Bennett and that American preacher lady." Cook's tone spoke volumes on her opinion of preacher ladies. "It's against nature, that's what it is, but that's none of our business." A more astute listener might have smiled at this remark. Cook continued, "Go an' gie that Raja a shout, an' I'll get him started cleanin' the silverware. Then he can cook that funny rice stuff they want for dinner. Things are gettin' a bit too fancy nowadays. Gie me the days o' meat an tatties an' two veggies, wi' somethin' sweet for afters, instead o' that highfalu-tin curry to burn your stomach awaw! I wonder what next?" These remarks expected and received no answer, as Betsy was on her way to find Raju.

"Raja, Raja. Where can he be, I wonder?" Raising her voice as she reached the foot of the attic stairs, Betsy rested for a minute before attempting to climb up. Her thoughts were busy on Cook's remarks about the changes. She was right, of course. Things were indeed a lot different now from the days when Mr. Blair and Mr. MacAlister would dash up and down these same stairs, two and three at a time, and—

"Betsy, have you nothing better to do than stand dreaming here on the bottom stair? I would have thought Cook would be able to keep you busy today."

"Oh, Mistress MacIntyre, Cook sent me to look for Raja, but I don't think he's in the house. He doesna' answer when I shout on him."

"Miss Gordon took him with her when she went in Paddy's brougham on some errands for me. I'll send him to the kitchen when they return. You get back to work, Betsy. We've all a busy evening ahead, so carry on."

"Yes, mistress." Betsy bobbed and turned quickly to make her way back to the kitchen. *What next indeed?* as Cook would say.

Beulah MacIntyre had also spent most of the day wondering. In fact, during the past few months, Beulah wondered about many things. Bad enough to wonder if she had failed her darling Jean, but what if she had been instrumental in driving her into the arms of the wrong man? Not that Jean complained. Oh, no, far from it; in fact she protested too much the other way, saying everything was fine. But many years of correspondence with her had given the grandmother an ability to read between the lines, and what she read she did not like. On the surface the most recent letter appeared to relate a nice story but. . . . Beulah had read it over dozens of times, and each time her uneasiness grew. She pulled it out again now.

Dear Granny: Thank you for the lovely letter and the lavender sachets. I'm sure the postie thinks I'm a fallen woman for receiving so many exotic fragrances in the post. Last week the packet of spices from Raju and this week your so lovely parcel.

All the villagers are characters, and I'm sure I've told you of Lachlan MacLachlan, the postie. Can you believe such a name?

Beulah paused now to gaze out the window as the writing grew blurred before her misting eyes. "Yes!" cried her heart to that faraway island. "Yes, my Jeannie, you told me about Lachlan, not once but many times." She wiped her eyes and continued to read:

And then there's the beadle, Wattie. He also goes round with a horse and van. He sells everything, and that means *everything*. He also sings! Oh, sorry, I should've said he's the cantor! We don't sing in our highland kirk. I suspect Wattie would like to, though. I mentioned that to Bruce the other day, but he didn't seem to agree with me. Very serious matters have to be considered when a new minister comes to a parish, and I suspect even Bruce didn't know how *serious* it all is. But he told me not to worry my head about anything except the "Women's Guild." When I explained to him that Mrs. Davidson had that well in hand—and I must confess, just to you, Granny, that I would be afraid to suggest anything at all to Mrs. Davidson—Bruce laughed, but I've noticed him turning a bit pale when she speaks to him.

You asked me about the manse, well, Granny, it's a dear, wee cottage and quite new really. It's the kirk that is two hundred years old. You would thrill at the sense of history about some of the old stone crosses and monuments. Faye Felicity will be pleased, as you will be, too, I hope, that I've started my book on that subject. The Standing Stones I mean, not Faye Felicity. I've mixed this all up again, so don't show it to anyone else, as I know you will understand.

Again Beulah stopped reading to dab with her lavender hankie before continuing. Yes, she understood only too well. Back to the letter:

Of course we want you all to come and see us. Keep up your prayers that things will improve for Bruce. He is so full of zeal and the desire to start a revival here on the Isle of Skye and then across the whole northwest, but I fear his efforts are not appreciated, as most of the folks don't think they need a revival. That is when he starts to get impatient. The old stones and other artifacts give one the impression that nothing has changed in a thousand years, and what do Bruce and Jean MacAlister think they can, or need, do to change what has survived so well for so long? I tried to tell Bruce my thoughts on this, too, but he got angry. He is right, of course. I must mind only my own part as the minister's wife, especially in my "delicate condition." Well I must draw to a close now.

Reading this over, I wonder if I should even post it, since it seems so full of complaining and criticizing, but believe me, Granny, it must be my "condition," because I have no cause whatever to complain. We are *deliriously* happy in our love cottage. People are so kind and generous to us.

Dr. Lockhart says I have the constitution of an ox and will be just fine when the time comes. I'm not sure if that's a compliment, but I think he meant it to be. Anyway, the midwife, Mrs. Armstrong, was trained in the William Simpson Memorial Maternity Pavilion, in Edinburgh, and she lives only two houses from the manse. Truly, things could not be better. Make plans to come after the "event." Give my love to everyone at Strathcona House.

Jean

Dropping the dog-eared sheets onto her lap, Beulah sat for a long time, contemplating what she had done to bring this all to pass. During the few months immediately after the reception, when Bruce had been finishing out his curateship here in Glasgow, it had seemed as if Jean were never off the doorstep. The Gorbals, an undesirable section of the city, to be sure, was nevertheless so close by that on Fridays, when Bruce brought Jean to spend the day with her, it had been wonderful. She came to with a start as Faye Felicity entered her room.

"Nothing in today's post, Auntie?" Faye Felicity knew the answer to her question. If a letter had arrived, the whole household would know by now. Agatha Rose joined the other two women as Beulah repeated the answer, used every day now. "No, my dear, but we must make allowances, a busy minister's wife and in her condition, too. Did you bring the lace?"

"Yes, and the other items are being delivered. I do think it an excellent idea to have a dress made up for Jean. The ones she made for herself to take to Inverechny seemed too dark and heavy for a girl like our Jean. Surely she cannot refuse to wear the cream brocade when it is given as a lying-in gift. This dusky rose lace goes very nicely with the sample. I'm so glad, for our sakes, too, that the new styles are straighter in the skirt and above the ankles. How I've always hated to sweep the street with our long crinolines." Agatha Rose stared at her aunt. Such a long speech was most unusual. Catching a warning glance and the merest shake of the head, she joined in the talk about the fashions.

"I'm glad, too, and I know Gran'ma Gordon will be. Why, when we stayed at their farm last summer, we got to wear trews when we helped with the hay and—"

"I would request that you refrain from wearing trews in the town of Glasgow, Aggie, my dear." But Beulah smiled as she spoke: "That frock you have on today is lovely, so light and it makes you look more like a rose than ever. Your coloring allows you to wear that bright pink admirably, whereas my Jean shouldn't wear pink at all, with her red hair." Suddenly, to the utter amazement of her listeners, the indomitable Auntie Mac began to weep. Faye Felicity ran to her, and Agatha stepped back uncertainly.

"What is it, Auntie? You've not had bad news?"

"No! No! Faye Felicity. I'm a silly, imagining old Granny, that's what I am. But it's so unlike my Jeannie, and I blame myself for almost pushing her at that young man. Oh, I could have taken an oath that he cared for her and would be good to her and now. . . . But I should not be behaving or speaking like this, I. . . ."

"Aggie, go and find some clean hankies and tell Betsy to bring tea." When the door closed behind an extremely relieved Aggie, Faye Felicity turned back to Beulah. "Now! What is all this about blaming yourself? You know as well as I do that nothing on earth would have kept that young lady from having Bruce MacAlister. Why the first time she saw him, her mind, and yes, her heart, became fixed on him. We also know that he is a good man and that he loves her. I believe at this stage he is both bewildered and overwhelmed with the circumstances of life. He is experiencing a stage of, well the Americans have a saying that is most descriptive, 'stuffed shirt'! I would call it the Pharisee stage myself, but I would add, 'This, too, shall pass.' Think of all he has been asked to do in this last year." Beulah had stopped sobbing, and the younger woman had her full attention. "Ordination, marriage, a most difficult curacy. He has a disapproving mother to consider, to say nothing of his in-laws. Remember what happened with Colonel Irvine at Jean's coming out? He has a first parish, not the choicest in the world, if one can read between the lines of Jean's letters. He is an expectant father; I don't believe men are given much consideration for their sufferings in this delicate condition, and he is altogether a very serious man. Now it is my prediction that the minute the child is born, everything will change, and Bruce MacAlister's true nature will come through again!" As Faye Felicity finished her second long speech within the hour, her old friend nodded in glad agreement.

"Of course, of course! Forgive me my moment of weakness. Faye Felicity, you have put into words what we know but had forgotten. Most important, God is on the throne and will take care of her. Now we will spend the next few weeks stitching the dress for Jean. By then the baby will have arrived. Then we will make the journey to the wilds of Skye, taking the box of baby gifts." The two sat in companionable silence for a time, until Beulah again spoke. "Oh, I do feel much better, and here comes Betsy with tea. After we drink it, we must hurry and prepare for our guests. Do the Americans really have a saying 'stuffed shirt'? It is so apt. Oh, Faye Felicity?" If Agatha Rose had been astonished to see Auntie MacIntyre in tears before, her stunned relief when she reentered the room to see and hear this hilarity was beyond description. The expression on Aggie's face caused a fresh burst of laughing and stopped only when she, summoning all the dignity she could muster, queried, "Shall I pour the tea, Auntie Mac? And could you share the fun? I would like a laugh, too."

Despite Cook's apprehensions about the food, the company was delighted with it all, especially the lady preacher. Dark, flaky rice, steaming with exotic fragrances, new to her nose and palate and served with crisp, flat cakes of bread which one dipped in a dish of steaming fragrant ragout appealed to Amelia. At a signal from the hostess, Raju Singh, beautifully turned out in his best scarlet and gold livery, complete with tasseled turban from the Punjab days, had given a demonstration of how to eat without cutlery and without spills. After some false starts, Amelia had managed to convey the food to her mouth, without too many dips in the finger bowl at her elbow. Dear George did not fare so well and finally was laughingly presented with a spoon.

When Beulah MacIntyre rose to lead her company to the sitting room, the gentlemen followed. If Colonel Irvine had been somehow able to view this procession, with his Indian servant being accorded such a place of honor by his wife's mother, he truly would have had an apoplectic fit.

Assuring herself the guests were looking after themselves admirably, Beulah turned to her friend George Bennett, their subject a certain manse in a far-off misty isle.

·─·❀{ 23 }❀·─·

"**O**f course I need to go, Jean! You know there are times when a minister has to answer a sickbed call the same as a doctor has to, and his family must take second place to the needs of his flock." Reaching into the cupboard for his thick jersey as he spoke, Bruce failed to see the glance of utter despair on his wife's face.

"Oh, Bruce, it's just that I feel a bit sick, and the time is near, and oh, darling, don't leave me now, I'm frightened." She went to him and awkwardly tried to put her arms round his neck. He removed them gently.

"Jean, this man is dying, and Mistress Armstrong said Dr. Lockhart told her he won't last much longer. If that's the case, and this Mr. Wilson is not ready for eternity, we would never forgive ourselves for being so self-indulgent in this hour. Now, if you're that frightened, I'll fetch Mistress Armstrong, and when I see Dr. Lockhart at the Wilson croft, I'll tell him, too. But remember what he said last time we sent for him. It was a false alarm, and a first bairn takes a long while."

"I know, and he thinks it will be at least three weeks yet, maybe more. I'm sorry, Bruce. Go on your mission of mercy, but be careful. The storm sounds worse, and the seas will be heavy at the Lang Ford." Feelings should not be trusted at such times, Jean assured herself.

"I'll be careful, and the Lang Ford isn't that long, you know.

Ten minutes in the ferry boat, compared to five hours on horseback to go round by land. Stop worrying, Jean, and start praying that our mission to save souls, this old man Wilson included, will be blessed. It's all in the Lord's hands anyway. We both know the day of miracles is not past, and the Lord who calmed the Sea of Galilee can calm a wee passage of water on the Isle of Skye, in Scotland." He had been pulling on his fisherman's hip waders as he spoke, and picking up his cap, he paused before opening the door to face the dark, threatening night. Unable to keep up her aloofness, Jean moved to him again. Not risking her voice, she clasped him tightly round the waist and hung on. Again he gently disengaged her hands. Bending, he planted a kiss on her tear-wet cheeks.

"I'll be home again before long, you'll see." He quickly pulled the door shut behind him, and she was alone.

Choking back a final plea, Jean whispered to the cosy room. "Did you say you would get Mistress Armstrong or not?" As if on signal, a sharp pain coursed through her body. "Oh, no, oh, please God, let me wait until he comes back!"

When Dr. Lockhart first told Jean she could expect her baby in the early spring, her joy had known no bounds. However, when she had told Bruce and his enthusiasm had not matched hers, and she had asked him if he was truly happy about it, he had only said, "If God wills it, I will it!" Thinking of that day now as she held on to the mantle, trying to ignore what she knew in her heart to be no false alarm, Jean MacAlister smiled grimly. This great man of God that she had married, almost at gunpoint, was beginning to sound like the Grand Panjandrum himself. Other instances of this stuffiness came to her now.

"I'm the head of this household!" was his answer one day when she suggested that maybe he should have a life-insurance policy. He had continued, "I'll hear no more of that business, and I'll go this very day to tell the man who spoke to you about it that he is infringing upon his rights as an elder." He had marched straight over to the Johnstone residence without finishing his dinner, and soon the word was all over Inverechny. In spite of Jean's attempts to smooth ruffled feathers, the Johnstones had started going to the Lang Ford Kirk. Between pains now, Jean began to laugh at herself. Only Raju would enjoy that silly joke about the Panjandrum. The thought seemed disloyal to her beloved, so she immediately rebuked it, but she continued to pray as she remembered the sequel to the insurance-policy argument.

Bravely she had tackled him. "Darling, if you are going to be upset with your parishioners each time a small matter like this comes along, we will soon have no one left in the pews at all!" Looking up from his Bible reading, the familiar furrows threading his brows, he had carefully marked the place before closing the book.

"Jean, this is no small matter. I will explain once and for always. If and when I decide upon a life-insurance policy, I certainly will not get it from someone who creeps about behind my back and tries to intimidate my wife into something that is none of her concern."

"But Bruce, it *is* my concern."

"The subject is not open for debate, Jean. My decision is final. I do not intend to justify it."

"Oh, Bruce!" Her whole being yearned toward him as she cried out, "I thought we would be on an equal partnership."

"Not so. The Bible says the man is the head of the woman and the woman must submit!"

"But it also says—"

Picking up his Bible, he had interrupted her again, "No further discussion!" That had been six months ago.

Another spasm shot through her, and she bit hard on her knuckle to keep from screaming out her next prayer. "God, help me in the future to appreciate my husband's sterling qualities and encourage him through this most challenging pastorate, until he learns to laugh again. In the meantime I pray those qualities made him tell Mistress Armstrong."

To give Bruce his due, he had indeed tried to reach the midwife.

"If the storm keeps comin' on, she'll stay till mornin' at Ochilriggs. A bairn is due there, and they need her as well," announced Mr. Armstrong. For a space of ten seconds, Bruce hesitated as the midwife's husband continued to speak, "Is Mistress MacAlister thinkin' she's at her time then?"

Bruce called back over his shoulder, "Send Mistress Armstrong to assure my wife, the minute she returns. I'm off to the Lang Ford on an urgent call."

Shaking his head knowingly towards the sky, now entirely black and forbidding, Jock Armstrong called out, "Dinna go ower the Ford this night. It can be. . . ." The wind caught his words and whistled them away. If Bruce MacAlister heard, he did not heed.

"Must be a saint or a fool, the same ilt as the doctor!" soliloquized Jock as he shut the door firmly against the storm.

Striding his way toward the landing, Bruce suffered a few moments of anguish, and his heart quailed within. *What if?* and, *Maybe I should have stayed!* He knew some women used their "condition" to get their own way, but he was sure Jean would not try to keep him from his duty by such a method. Sternly he reaffirmed his resolve. He was committed, and even if her labor was real, women managed these things better with the men out of the way. Besides, Jock Armstrong had assured him he would send Mistress MacRae, a neighbor who assisted the midwife on occasion, to sit with Jean.

The man hailing him from the cockleshell boat, aggrandized by the term *ferry boat,* had a strangely familiar appearance. The scene in his home was quickly placed at the back of his mind as Bruce stared at the ferryman. Could it be possible?

"Hamish Cormack? Is it yourself? Where is old Colin Mac-Nab? I'm not believin' my eyes, and yet I would know you anywhere. Are you takin' Colin's place?"

"What for all the questions? Colin's awa' the now, an' I'm takin' his place right enough, but ma name's *Hector Dermott.* Who are you?"

"You may say you're Hector Dermott, but I know better.

You're my long-lost stepbrother. I'm Bruce MacAlister. But Hamish, what—"

"Whateffer are ye talkin' aboot, man? Are we to staun' here gabbin' aw nicht? Or did you want to get across to the other side afore the storm gets ony worse?"

"Now I'm certain you're Hamish. But, yes, I do need to cross the sound. I'm a minister, an' I've a sick call. Can we go quickly?" Climbing into the flimsy boat, he said, "My, this boat doesn't seem very sturdy, are you sure it'll carry us?"

"She's sturdier nor she looks, but if you don't hurry up, I'll change my mind and no' take her oot The weather changes quick at this time o' year, an' I'm hopin' it'll no get worse." Bruce settled into the middle of the passenger side, and the cockleshell dipped dangerously as he moved. Concentrating on sitting still, and praying hard, Bruce was surprised when he felt the boat scrape bottom on the opposite shore.

He jumped out, and the other man called after him. "Half an hour is all I'll wait. The signs are tellin' me the northeaster is a big blow, in fact, a twister. If we're caught in this channel in a twister, it turns into a boiler!"

Bruce ran up the shingle, but before he reached the road, the figure of Dr. Lockhart, stumbling and slipping down the rugged path, came into view. He was followed by a stout young fellow carrying a lantern. Dr. Lockhart shouted at Bruce, "It's yersel', reverend? Well, ye're too late for Duncan Wilson, I'm sorry to say. He went on to his reward, or punishment, whatever the case may be. I said a few words o' prayer masel'. He seemed happy enough to go. The pain must've been hard to thole."

At the word *pain* Bruce groaned aloud. "I'm sorry I was too late, doctor, but now I have to take you to my wife. She seemed to think her time was upon her." The doctor laughed without mirth as they made their careful way back to the primitive ferry landing.

"The first ones are often like that. As I told her—and

you—last week, she has at least a fortnight to go, but birth and death cannot be bidden. Both in the hands of the Lord. Eh, reverend? Anyway I'll look in on her before I go home, just to make sure." A shiver ran through Bruce as he listened to the doctor, and it was nothing to do with the cold.

"I'd be much obliged, Dr. Lockhart." They had come to the beached boat, and an agitated boatman, whom Bruce knew to be Hamish Cormack, yelled, "I can only take one o' ye and come back for the other. Stop gabbin' and hurry."

"You go, doctor, and please go straight to my wife. The skimpy boat disappeared into the gloom. Dropping to his knees on the pebbly shore, Bruce prayed. "Dear Father in heaven, you know I'm just beginning in my work for you, but I see where I've been wrong with Jean. Oh, please, God, help me through these next few hours, and spare Jean. I promise I'll do better." The age-old cry echoed back to him as the wind surged ever stronger. "I'll serve you more as Gran'pa Bruce showed me and less as this Bruce has come to think or as the university taught me. God help me!"

"Aye, God help you, all right, an' me as weel. Get in the boat quick. I must be daft to have come back for you!" Bruce rose from his knees. Did the storm seem to be dying down? It occurred to him that maybe he was turning all this into high drama, what with Jean's emotional outburst and then meeting Hamish and the deathbed that he never did reach. Hamish must have rowed across this short strip of water many times and would not have risked coming back for him, if they were in deadly peril.

"You need not make a mockery of the name of God, Hamish, and as you can see, the storm is dying down."

"The storm's gettin' faint, aye, but sometimes it's cheatin' an' lulls for a wee while then can come back worse. Curses on ye, sur, reverend or no', ma name's no' *Hamish*, it's *Hector*, and if you're prayin', pray that the lull lasts till we're ower on the other side."

"Hamish, thank you for coming back. You've guessed by now my wife may be in travail!"

"Aye. Well, that's your worry an' no' mine. I'll be chargin' you two pounds extra for the risk." The small craft moved out into the open water.

Ashamed of his outburst, Bruce took a minute to consider the situation. If he became this fearful every time an emergency arose, his ministry would be ineffective and his dreams of revival among his own people would come to nothing. He must learn to control his emotions in a crisis.

A shout from Hamish brought his full attention to the present situation. "It's the twister! See yon wave? If I can turn the boat so's we go wi' it, we micht be fine, but if it catches us broadside we're a—" The giant wave engulfed the slight boat before Hamish finished speaking, and within seconds it was smashed like an eggshell in a giant fist. Bruce gasped as the icy water swept over him. Down, down he went, arms flailing wildly. Almost immediately his head was above water, and he grabbed at a plank from the boat as it raced by him. Something larger brushed past his face, and he let go of the wood to clasp at the inert figure of his stepbrother. Responding instinctively, Bruce became oblivious to time or anything else except the immediate need.

24

The blackness was complete. Bruce, seeing no lights anywhere, no sign of land or indeed anything except the wall of water against which he could do nothing, relaxed, merely allowing it to take them as he assured himself the other man's head kept uppermost. Finally Bruce managed to hitch the unconscious Hamish underneath his arm and attempted to swim. Finding it impossible, he ceased struggling.

The freezing water numbed him, but he stayed quiet within his spirit, knowing that nothing less than a miracle would save them. He prayed for it as his Gran'pa Bruce had taught him: "Father God, we need a miracle, if it be Thy will, Lord, spare us now. I cannot understand any of this, but save Hamish, too, dear Lord. My life is Yours at any rate, and whatever it is You ask of me, I will work twice as hard to do. As for Hamish here, I'll tell him about You. Save his life and his soul, please, God. Nothing's too hard for You, Lord, and it is so cold in this water, and I need to get back to Jean. All the promises I've made this night I'll keep, with Your help. Jesus, could you just warm up my blood so's my legs'll be none the worse, and could you channel some heat to Hamish, too?"

Josiah Burns and his wife, Sarah, welcomed the twisters, at least the after crops. More profitable than the fishing was the salvaging of driftwood and other valuable rubbish washed up on the stretch of shore in front of their lean-to. The daft southerners would pay good siller for any old bits of wood that came up off the wrecks of ancient Stuart galley ships known to be sunken hereabouts. Last night's twister had been a dandy.

"See that ower there, Sarey. Is yon a good bit o' an auld ship or . . .?" Sarah shaded her eyes. The glorious, rain-washed Hebridean sunrise went unnoticed in their quest for spoil.

"If it is, it's shurely a big enough bit, Josiah. We'll gang closer an' hae a better look." Closer inspection showed not a piece of a ship but two bodies entwined and lying completely without movement. Sarah shrieked. "It's two deed men. Come awa', Josiah!" But her husband, made of sterner stuff, started to run and was soon bending over the find.

"They're no' deed, Sarey! The big yin onyway is breathin'!"

"Come awa' Josiah, the de'il take them if he it is that washed them oot o' a twister like yon."

Josiah laughed nervously. "Dinna be daft, wumman, the big fella here is dressed in fine woolen claes wi' a meenister's collar underneath, forby. So we'll tak' them ben the hoose an' get them dried an' gie them a hot drink and. . . ."

Sarah's own good sense returned as she, too, saw the possibilities.

"Ye're right enuff, Josiah, a guid-hearted man as well. This should be wurth mair than a bit driftwood."

An entirely different Hamish, a Hamish who would learn in time the term "a new creature," awoke on the strange bed of skins and rags, only knowing from primitive instinct that his life no longer belonged to him. He looked round for Bruce. Not finding him, he struggled to sit up. The woman scolded him to lie down again, as his head had a lump the size of a hen's egg, and he was suffering from chills.

Ignoring her, he asked, "Where's my brother?"

Josiah Burns, who had seen this man going about the docks in Portree and knew him for a scrounger like himself, jeered, "Your brother? Aye, and Bonnie Prince Chairlie's ma cousin."

Hamish climbed off the bed. His jacket and boots had been removed, but he strode over to the peat fireplace, where they steamed on the tin fender. Without another word, he pulled on the damp boots and stamped out.

Sarah yelled after him, "Some gratitude for us who dragged you from a watery grave!"

"You'll be paid," he called back as he stepped out briskly in the general direction of Inverechny.

Recovering his senses at the same moment as Josiah, who was accustomed to moving much heavier objects, had begun the process of dragging his inert frame across the sand, Bruce had leaped to his feet. Stopping only to assure himself that Hamish lived, he had pushed aside every obstacle until he reached his home and ran into the room where his wife lay. He had thrown himself to the floor beside the bed and clasped the small, pale hand that hung limply on top of the counterpane.

"Oh, Jean, my dearest love. I'm sorry! Forgive me. Come back to me. I need you!" The midwife, at the doorway and ready to announce the arrival of Dr. Lockhart, had stopped in her tracks. She glanced at the doctor, and the two retreated wordlessly. This was the very best kind of healing.

When, a few hours later, Hamish Cormack, too, reached the manse, Armstrong's wife told him of the night's happenings there. He settled down quietly for a time of watching and waiting while the MacAlisters, now numbering three, slept the sleep of utter exhaustion.

Meanwhile the differing versions of the night's events spread, reaching the public house at Lang Ford, and lost nothing at each telling. Lachlan MacLachlan's many listeners marveled as the postman related how the young minister's wife had nearly died in childbed and that the minister himself, out answering a deathbed call, had almost drowned, the ferryman with him. By then the crowd in Charlie's Arms had multiplied, and when Josiah Burns entered for his hour of triumph, the crowd milled round him. Lachlan left to return to Inverechny, and the beachcomber had the floor, with none to gainsay him.

A bearded drinker threw a question at Josiah, "You say you saw them comin' oot the watter?"

"Saw them, man! They were walkin' on the watter!"

A hush fell on the listeners. Josiah was not known for his honesty, but again, no one could have spent more than an hour or two in that freezing water in the middle of a twister and survived, not without other than human aid. A shiver ran through the listeners as the innkeeper posed another question, "One o' them was Hector Dermott, you say?"

"Aye, but the big one called him Hamish. He must've been runnin' the ferry for Colin." Looks were exchanged, and the landlord laughed.

"Hamish? There's nae ferryman hereaboots wi' the name o' Hamish."

"I only said the big one ca'ed him that."

"Lachlan says it was the new meenister fae Inverechny."

"If he did walk on the watter, then I'm for goin' to that kirk an' see whit it's a' aboot." The laughter following this remark had a hollow ring, though, and soon the pub emptied of all but Josiah and the landlord.

"Have another drap, Josiah. . . . He really walked on the watter then?" Samuel Todd was a foreigner from over Aberdeen way, and although he had lived and served the people of Lang Ford for forty years, he would ever be a foreigner. But he knew his highland customers well. "Drink up, man, whilest I get a letter ready to post to my brother. He writes the news for the Inverness *Courier*, and I'm sure he'll be interested in what you have to say."

On a Wednesday morning two months later, Dugald the Post was on his rounds early. Finished in Aribaig, he made his way to the Mains Farm at a half-run, half-walk, stopping only once at the bridge to catch his breath. In his pouch three letters rested. One from Mrs. Cormack to Andrew, one from Glasgow, he suspected from the auld granny there, and one strange envelope. Dugald knew his envelopes well, and this one was fancy: thick, handmade vellum, embossed with the one word, *Munro*, and postmarked *Edinburgh*. Only one thing wrong with that one. It was addressed to Mrs. Elspeth MacAlister, so he wouldn't find out what it was about today. But here was Andrew coming to meet him, and the tea would be made. Without the mistress, the baking was not the same, but Mrs. MacDonald did her best, and he'd make sure her scones had a fair sampling. Gran'pa Bruce came round the corner of the steading, followed by an excited dog or two. They trooped into the warm, waiting kitchen together. Now for the news. Andrew cleared his throat, glancing round the table before beginning:

Dear Husband, Gran'pa, and Dugald, too:
    This letter is to tell you that I'll be home next week! As you said, Andrew, the longer I stay here the harder it is to think of leaving this wee one. She is so good and clever. Never was a bairn this age so canny!

Andrew chuckled, and the others joined in as he continued,

    Again you were right, Andrew. The bairn does make a difference to my thoughts on Bruce's marrying Jean. . . .

"Or onybody!" This from Dugald, and Bruce, Senior, nodded while saying, "Weesht, man! Go on, Andrew."

    The days are warm and long. I just put a line of nappies and things out to blow in that fine breeze from the sea. The village is settling down from all that talk of miracles, and I just hope the kirk will, too. Anyway the reporters have long since disappeared.
    Our son gave a braw sermon yesterday. A wee touch radical maybe, but I see some of Gran'pa Bruce and some

of Fraser as well as his own self, which is the uppermost, and we can all be proud of him.

About Jean, she is gaining slowly but surely. The doctor let her up for a while this morning, and Bruce carried her out to sit in the sun. She's a bonnie lassie for all her red hair!

The sigh from Andrew was echoed by the other men, and Andrew choked a bit before going on.

She's strong-willed, mind you, and not out of the woods yet, but she'll do. I must stop the writing and get on with the other jobs. I'll write again on Friday. . . .

Elspeth Cormack

P.S. Hamish is a new man altogether. He says his life now belongs to Bruce as well as Jesus! We'll see! EMC.

Mrs. MacDonald replenished the tea cups, announcing: "If you're needin' onything else, gie me a shout. I'll get on wi' the cleanin'." Andrew absently waved the letter. "Aye, Mrs. Mac-Donald. Ye heard the mistress will be hame next week?"

"I did, and I heard the ither guid news, too."

Gran'pa opened the letter from Glasgow and began to read.

Dear Mr. MacAlister:

Thank you for the letter with your views about Bruce and Jean. I find you a most discerning gentleman, and I value your opinion. When I, being in such a state when we last met, allowed my feelings to sway my better judgment and my tongue, I deserved more than your gentle admonishment. I'm glad you are a forgiver You remind me that our young couple have a long, possibly hard, road yet to travel, but that is life itself, is it not? The boating accident and the subsequent miracle (we both give God the true credit for this, don't we?) brought Bruce to his knees and his senses. Jean, touching death's door and almost going to be present with the Lord, is also a different girl, more mature and a true woman now, and has advanced far in her thinking. My fears for them have vanished, thank God! As for wee Mary Jean, she is destined for something very special, isn't she?

You kindly asked about the other extensions of my family. I have heard from Jean's mother that her husband, Cameron, is very ill. He suffers from liver complaint. Only God, by His Spirit, can give me the compassion I need for that man. Join me in prayer that he and Jessica, my daughter, will find Christ before it's too late.

Young Peter, or I should say Dr. Peter Blair, is seriously courting Agatha Rose Gordon, my friend's niece, enough so that she will stay here with me instead of going to Calcutta. You made their acquaintance at the reception here in Strathcona House. Peter is going to church regularly, and after a visit from Aggie's father, he is off the "demon drink," we pray for good. I believe it. He is also taking instruction on the Book from Mr. George Bennett. Again I say, "Thank God!"

Raju Singh left for Calcutta immediately upon his return from Inverechny, where he assured himself that Jean, Bruce, and baby Mary Jean didn't need him anymore. He and Faye Felicity traveled on the same boat, as she is for the mission field there. . . .Well, my friend, time to close. I will be pleased to hear from you again. I enjoy reading of your thoughts on John the Divine and his Revelation. They concur very closely to the teachings of my late husband.

Yours in Christ,
Beulah MacIntyre

The farm cart rocked dangerously, and Andrew made his usual remark that one of these days they would invest in a "jauntin' car," but Elspeth paid him no heed as she stared at the strange yet all too familiar letter from Edinburgh. Andrew waited for as long as he could before saying, "Well, wife, read it! Read it!" Slowly she removed the double sheets from the envelope.

Elspeth, my dear daughter:

It is more than I deserve that you would ever call me Mother again, although of course that is who I am. My cowardly behavior does not change the fact. I am still a coward and only write because your father is in no condition to stop me from communicating with you or, for that matter, from doing anything I wish. He has been rendered helpless by, what the doctor describes as a massive stroke. I would like to say there is hope for him, but I fear there is none, either for his body or his soul!

Elspeth glanced at Andrew. He had loosed his grip on the reins, and the horse ambled to the verge to nibble the grass. Andrew's eyes were closed, so she went on.

Recently I saw an article in the *Times* about a Reverend Bruce MacAlister! Could you write and tell me if this is who I think it is? My one and only grandson. I will await your reply and beg your indulgence in this.

Meanwhile, may I ask you and your family to pray for your father? His physician, along with the specialist brought in for a second opinion, says he is conscious of everything in and around him. Can you imagine his feelings when he is no longer in control of himself?

Strangely, or maybe not so strangely, I seem to have taken on a new lease of life, making decisions and literally rising from a sickbed of my own making to take up the reins. What can be considered strange is I bear no vindictiveness toward him, only the same terrible sorrow I've always felt and that he would hate, if he knew.

Several possibilities present themselves to me now. The first one is to visit the place in Skye where Bruce is and subsequently to come and see you, if you will have me Dare I hope? Because I still am

Your loving Mother

A thrush trilled its song of joy from a nearby lone tree as the two in the ancient vehicle gazed at each other. Andrew smiled faintly, waiting for some kind of outburst from his wife, but she turned tear-filled eyes on him. He moved toward her and held her tightly for a time. Then, clucking to the horse to start moving again, he said, "Our Bruce was always taken up with the 'islands of the sea,' but I'm thinking now of the islands within people. We're all islands in a sea with ripples going in and around us. This old man, Hugh Munro, is an island indeed and in the most grim of fortresses. Only God, in His infinite mercy, can broach it. Aye, yes, Elspeth, we'll pray for him, for his mind, soul and body. God is able! Meanwhile, wife, write and tell your mother to come, after she's been to Inverechny. I believe Bruce will guide her as to what she would do now, until she finds out for herself that, like you and Bruce and any others who have been damaged by your father, she, too, must forgive him. He's a poor soul and always was, even in good health. Wipe your tears, wife, and read to me from the Book our son's favorite chapter in Isaiah."

Elspeth gave a final sniff before dazzling her husband with a smile. Picking up the worn Bible that went with Andrew everywhere, she read:

They shall lift up their voice, they shall sing for the majesty of the Lord, they shall cry aloud from the sea. Wherefore glorify ye the Lord in the fires, even the name of the Lord God of Israel in the isles of the sea.